Midsummer—A Natural Time of Ce

Every culture has, at some point in its history, marked the time of Midsummer and held it to be enchanted.

The Celts, the Norse, and the Slavs believed that there were three "spirit nights" in the year when magic abounded and the Otherworld was near. The first was Halloween, the second was May Eve, and the third was Midsummer Eve. On this night, of all nights, fairies are most active. As the solstice sun rises on its day of greatest power, it draws up with it the power of herbs, standing stones, and crystals. In the shimmering heat-haze on the horizon, its magical energies are almost visible.

The cold, dark days of winter and blight are far away, and the time of light and warmth, summer and growth, is here. We naturally feel more joyful and want to spend more time in the open air. The crops are planted and growing nicely, and the young animals have been born.

Midsummer is a natural time of celebration.

About the Author

Anna Franklin (England) has been a practicing Pagan for thirty years and a high priestess for fifteen, leading and organizing many Midsummer rites. She now works as a therapist, teacher, photographer, artist, and writer. She is also the author of *The Sacred Circle Tarot,* illustrated by Paul Mason; and coauthor, with Paul Mason, of *Lammas.*

To Write to the Author

If you wish to contact the author or would like more information about this book, please write to the author in care of Llewellyn Worldwide and we will forward your request. Both the author and publisher appreciate hearing from you and learning of your enjoyment of this book and how it has helped you. Llewellyn Worldwide cannot guarantee that every letter written to the author can be answered, but all will be forwarded. Please write to:

Anna Franklin
℅ Llewellyn Worldwide
P.O. Box 64383, Dept. 0-7387-0052-5
St. Paul, MN 55164-0383, U.S.A.

Please enclose a self-addressed stamped envelope for reply,
or $1.00 to cover costs. If outside U.S.A., enclose
international postal reply coupon.

Many of Llewellyn's authors have websites with additional information
and resources. For more information, please visit our
website at http://www.llewellyn.com.

MIDSUMMER

MAGICAL CELEBRATIONS
of the
SUMMER SOLSTICE

ANNA FRANKLIN

2003
Llewellyn Publications
St. Paul, Minnesota 55164-0383, U.S.A

First Edition
Second printing, 2003

Book design by Donna Burch
Cover art © 2001 by Jennifer Hewitson
Cover design by Kevin R. Brown
Editing by Andrea Neff
Interior illustrations © 2001 by Joanna Roy

Special thanks to Melissa Mierva for the herb precautions

Library of Congress Cataloging-in-Publication Data

Franklin, Anna.
    Midsummer : magical celebrations of the summer solstice / Anna Franklin.—1st ed.
      p.   cm.
    Includes bibliographical references and index.
    ISBN 0-7387-0052-5
      1. Summer solstice. 2. Summer festivals. 3. Neopaganism—Rituals. I. Title.
GT4995.S85 F73 2002
349.263—dc21   2001050702

Llewellyn Publications
A Division of Llewellyn Worldwide, Ltd.
P.O. Box 64383, Dept. 0-7387-0052-5
St. Paul, MN 55164-0383, U.S.A.
www.llewellyn.com

 Printed in the United States of America on recycled paper

Dedication

For Rachel, Amazon, and Nikki, the Flower Brides of Midsummer.

Acknowledgments

Thanks to Nancy Mostad, who has always been supportive, and to Andrea Neff and Donna Burch for their excellent work on this book. My thanks also to Nigel Pennick for his help on the vexed question of runes.

Other Works by Anna Franklin

Ritual Incenses and Oils

(Capall Bann, 2000)

The Wellspring

(Capall Bann, 2000)

Personal Power

(Capall Bann, 1998)

Pagan Feasts

(Capall Bann, 1997)

Lammas
with Paul Mason, coauthor

(Llewellyn, 2001)

Fairy Lore
with Paul Mason, Illustrator

(Capall Bann, 2000)

The Sacred Circle Tarot: A Celtic Pagan Journey
with Paul Mason, Illustrator

(Llewellyn, 1998)

The Fairy Ring: An Oracle of the Fairy Folk
with Paul Mason, Illustrator

(Llewellyn, 2002)

Real Wicca for Teenagers

(Capall Bann, 2002)

Contents

Chapter 5
Midsummer Herb Craft 91

Gathering Herbs for Magic • Drying Herbs • Special Uses for Herbs at Midsummer •
Incense • Magical Oils

Chapter 6
Traditional Midsummer Recipes 135

The Ritual of the Cakes and Wine • Coamhain Soup• Comfrey Fritters • Elderflower Fritters •
Gooseberry Fool • Elderflower Champagne • Anise Tea • Clary Sage Tea • Mint Tea •
Strawberry Wine • Black Mead • Sack • Heather Ale

Chapter 7
Midsummer Rituals 143

Basic Instructions for Indoor Rituals • Basic Instructions for Outdoor Rituals •
Rite for Midsummer • The Rite of the Oak King and the Holly King • Witch Rite for
Midsummer Day • Cornish Flower Ritual • Summer Lustration Ritual •
Drawing Down the Sun • Litha: A Saxon Midsummer Celebration •
Druidic Rite for Midsummer • Handfasting

Appendix 1
Animal Totems for Midsummer 175

Appendix 2
Midsummer Calendar 183

Appendix 3
Midsummer Correspondences 191

Appendix 4
Gods and Goddesses of Midsummer 195

Appendix 5
Sun Symbols 207

The Origins of the Midsummer Celebration

The celebration of Midsummer is a global custom. Every culture has, at some point in its history, marked this time of year and held it to be enchanted. The Celts, the Norse, and the Slavs believed that there were three "spirit nights" in the year when magic abounded and the Otherworld was near. The first was Halloween, the second was May Eve, and the third was Midsummer Eve. On this night, of all nights, fairies are most active, and the future can be uncovered. As the solstice sun rises on its day of greatest power, it draws up with it the power of herbs, standing stones, and crystals. In the shimmering heat-haze on the horizon, its magical energies are almost visible. And as the mist gate forms in the warm air rising beneath the dolmen arch, the entrance to the Otherworld opens— Avalon, Tir nan Og, the Land of Youth, where it is *always* summer, and

death and old age are unknown. Shakespeare captured all the magic of the occasion in *A Midsummer Night's Dream,* where fairies, magic, and mischief abound on one bewitched night in the forest.

Every ancient religion had its own customs and traditions associated with Midsummer. These appear in the lore of Greece and Rome, the myths of the Norse, the Maya, the Aztecs, the Slavs, and the Celts, the writings of the ancient Egyptians, and the Old Testament of the Jews. Vestiges of these festivities can still be witnessed today. In places we may still see the *baal* fires, the torchlight processions, the rolling of a sun wheel downhill, the casting of spells, divination, love magic, and the blessing of crops and animals with fire.

The cold, dark days of winter and blight are far away, and the time of light and warmth, summer and growth, are here. We naturally feel more joyful and want to spend more time in the open air. The crops are planted and growing nicely, and the young animals have been born.

Midsummer is a natural time of celebration.

The Four Solar Festivals

The festival is actually the observance of the summer solstice. There are two solstices annually. The summer solstice is the longest day of the year and falls around June 21 in the Northern Hemisphere and around December 21 in the Southern Hemisphere. The winter solstice is the shortest day of the year and falls around December 21 in the Northern Hemisphere and around June 21 in the Southern Hemisphere. The other two solar festivals are the equinoxes.

At the spring equinox, day and night are of equal length, but the light is gaining; the days are getting longer. Then at the summer solstice, the sun is at the height of its power on the longest day of the year. At the autumn equinox, day and night are again of equal length, but the dark is gaining; the days are getting shorter. At the winter solstice, the sun is at its weakest on the shortest day of the year.

The Technical Bit

The summer solstice marks the zenith of the sun, a time of greater warmth and longer hours of daylight. We experience changing seasons because the axis of the Earth—an imaginary line between the North and South Poles—is tilted from true by 23.5 degrees. As our planet revolves around the sun this means that part of the Earth tilts toward the sun, then away again. Between June and September the Northern Hemisphere is tilted toward the sun and gets more light, experiencing the season of summer. At the same time the Southern Hemisphere experiences winter. Between December and March the Northern Hemisphere is tilted away from the sun and receives less light and warmth, while the Southern Hemisphere enjoys summer. Just how much sunlight you receive depends on the latitude you occupy. By June 21 there are twenty-four hours of daylight above the Arctic Circle, while below the Antarctic Circle (which, if you remember, is experiencing the winter solstice) there are twenty-four hours of darkness. I am sure that you can work out the degrees of gradation between the two.

During spring and autumn both hemispheres experience milder weather, and the two equinoxes mark the junctures when the Earth's axis is pointing sideways. Without the tilt in the Earth's axis we would have the same degree of light and warmth—or dark and cold—all year round, and have no seasons at all; the sun's rays would always be directly over the equator.

The word *solstice* is derived from Latin and means "sun stands still." A little before and during the winter and summer solstices, the sun appears to rise and set at almost exactly the same place. The summer solstice is celebrated when the sun reaches its most northerly position. Throughout the year the sun passes through the constellations of the zodiac, and the summer solstice occurs in the constellation of Cancer, the Crab. If you have ever wondered why a zodiac sign should be named after a crab, it is because the sun seems to travel backward after this point in time every year, descending the zodiacal arch—just like a crab walking.

Midsummer in Prehistory

There is plenty of evidence that prehistoric people were fascinated by the passage of time. Thirty thousand years ago they were making tallies of the moon's phases on bone and horn sticks. These techniques gradually became more sophisticated and evolved into ways of marking the solstices and equinoxes, of predicting astronomical events and eclipses. Early on these may have been marked by an observer in a chosen position placing wooden posts or pegs where the sun rose and set at these times of year. Later on, stones would replace the pegs. By the New Stone Age (8,000 years ago), stone circles, like Stonehenge, were orientated to mark the position of the rising sun at the midsummer solstice. The sun would rise over a heel stone and cast a long, phallic shadow into the heart of the circle, consummating the marriage of heaven and earth.[1] Other circles mark the equinoxes and the cross-quarter festivals we know as Imbolc, Lughnasa, Beltane, and Samhain.

The great importance of these festivals to ancient people can be surmised when we realize that tons of stone was moved and raised without the aid of machinery—a process that must have been back-breaking work spanning many years.

Ancient China

In ancient China the summer solstice was accounted feminine and predominantly yin, a summer festival of earth and fertility. Offerings were made to encourage the fecundity of the earth. In contrast the winter solstice was accounted male, yang, and celestial. Offerings were burned so that their smoke would rise to the heavens.

Together the two solstices formed the balance of the year, summer and winter, female and male, earth and sky, light and dark, and the marriage of the two was symbolized by the famous yin/yang symbol.

The Celts and Druids

We know comparatively little about how the Pagan Celts celebrated their festivals, as they left no written records. What we do know comes from the later accounts of Christian monks, writing of traditions that they were in the act of suppressing. The monks thought it their duty to strip any traces of Paganism from what they wrote, transforming Pagan gods and goddesses into ordinary men and women, heroes, and even Christian saints. We have to carefully unravel real Pagan myths and traditions from the knotted tangle of the whole. Fortunately, a good indicator of what actually took place is the survival of ancient folklore customs in the Celtic countries. From these we can guess at some of the older festivals that lie behind them. Prevalent among these is the celebration of Midsummer, with bonfires on tops of hills and cairns. These hilltop fires are a central part of this celebration in many parts of the world, a symbolic encouraging of the fire of the sun with "little brother" bonfire, lit on a hill, and therefore in a place as near to the sky as possible.

The four Celtic festivals of Imbolc, Beltane, Lughnasa, and Samhain were based on the pastoral calendar and marked the activities of the shepherd and cowherd. The four festivals of the solstices and equinoxes relate not only to a solar calendar, but also to an agricultural one, marking crop-planting and harvesting times.

The druid priesthood were learned men and women who studied astronomy and carefully marked the solstices and equinoxes. At the summer solstice they celebrated the marriage of heaven and earth and kindled the sacred need fire of oak wood. They gathered their sacred herbs infused with the sun's power and dried them so that they were ready to use in magic and healing work. It was at this time of year that they gathered the mistletoe berries believed to turn golden for one night a year—at Midsummer. They believed that these berries, the fabled golden bough, had the power to cure all ills, containing as they do the seed of Midsummer fire.[2]

The Celts believed that there were two suns, the sun of the waxing year and the sun of the waning year. Traces of myths in many places of the world indicate two opposing rulers of the year, characterized as the light king and the dark king, or the Oak King and the Holly King. Midsummer was associated with the thunder god Taranis, king of the oak, who brings the summer rain.

The Northern Traditions

The Saxons began their year at the midwinter solstice, and the summer solstice marked its midpoint. They called the month of June *Aerra Litha,* meaning "before Litha," and July *Aeftera Litha,* meaning "after Litha."[3] This led some to speculate that the Saxon name for the festival was Litha, which is usually translated as "light" or perhaps "moon." J.R.R. Tolkien used this term for a midsummer festival in the fantasy novel *The Lord of the Rings*. At Midsummer, Thor, god of thunder, brought the rains.

The Germanic tribes marked the summer solstice with huge bonfires to salute the victory of the sun over darkness and death. With the Christianization of the area it became the Feast of St. John or Johannisnacht ("John's Night"). On St. John's Eve in Bavaria fires were lit on the mountains by shepherds, a custom dating back to Germanic tribal celebrations. Even today people make their way up to the hills to kindle fires of wood collected over the preceding weeks by the village children.

Midsummer was and still is an important festival for those who live in the far north. The light of midsummer is a great contrast to the long hours of darkness in the winter. The Finnish summer festival is called the *kesäjuhlat*. The house is thoroughly cleaned and birch trees are placed outside the front door. In ancient times there would have been feasting, dancing, bonfires, and offerings to the earth in the form of food placed on a sacred stone.[4]

In Iceland the year began on Midsummer Sunday, and the first month was called *Heyanír*, meaning "haytoil," since this is the time of haymaking.

Midsummer is celebrated all over Sweden. As in Finland, England, and Wales, Midsummer poles of birch are erected and decorated with flowers and greenery. Dancing takes place around the poles, which symbolize the marriage of earth and sky. There are seasonal songs and dances, and many parties and feasts. In some provinces a Midsummer Bride is chosen and crowned. She then chooses herself a Midsummer Bridegroom and a collection of money is made for the pair.[5]

Ancient Rome

The midsummer solstice was sacred to Juno, the queen of heaven and guardian of the female sex. She was the wife of Jupiter, a sky and thunder deity, chief of the gods. Juno was the patroness of marriage; the month of June is named after her, and it is still the most popular month for marriages. On this day, too, she is Juno Luna, the moon goddess who confers menstruation on women.[6]

The time of the midsummer solstice was also sacred to Vesta, goddess of the hearth fire. Earlier in the month her sanctuary doors were thrown open and the married women of Rome entered the temple to make offerings in the form of salted grain meal. The offerings went on for eight days, after which the temple was thoroughly cleansed.

The festival of the dawn goddess Mater Metuta was held in June. Women led female servants to her temple and then beat them with sticks. The time was also sacred to Venus, goddess of love.

The Roman writer Pliny advised farmers to light bonfires in the fields during the height of summer to ward off disease.[7]

Mesopotamia

The rites of the goddess Ishtar and her lover Tammuz were celebrated at Midsummer in the Middle East, though further north they were celebrated at the vernal equinox. The month of Tammuz corresponds to our June/July.

Ishtar loved Tammuz, the young vegetation god. He returned her love, but was tragically killed by a boar. The goddess was devastated and was determined to go to the underworld, ruled by her sister Ereshkigal, and bring him back. To do this she had to pass the seven gates of the underworld and at each surrender some article of her clothing and jewelry. Finally she stood before her sister naked and vulnerable. The queen of the underworld was unmoved and imprisoned Ishtar also.

Without Tammuz and Ishtar the world became a barren desert and the other gods became alarmed. The gods of the sun and moon appealed to Ea, the god of water and magic, for help. He sent a messenger to the underworld with a powerful magic spell, and the two were immediately released. He purified the young god and goddess with water, and the earth became fertile once more.

This myth tells of the barren months when the sun is too hot and the rains are withheld and no crops can grow. Only the god of water can free the harvest god from the underworld and make the seeds shoot.

The Greeks

In Italy and Greece, Tammuz became Adonis ("Lord"). In the heat of summer the women planted small pots of fast-growing plants called *Gardens of Adonis*, which were allowed to grow and wither in the space of a few days before being thrown into the sea.

For the ancient Greeks the day was sacred to all high priestesses and *heras*, the female guardians of temples and communities. The name is derived from the goddess Hera, wife of the chief god Zeus (a sky/thunder deity) and the Greek equivalent of the Latin Juno. In another sense a hera is a human being who has achieved union with the Mother of All Things.[8] The male equivalent is *hero*. The name of the hero Herakles (Hercules) means "beloved of Hera."[9] Herakles' famous twelve labors represent the passage of the sun through the twelve signs of the zodiac during a solar year.

Athene (Athena), goddess of wisdom, has solar characteristics. The Greek year began on the first new moon after the solstice with a Panathenaia festival in her honor. This was celebrated as the birthday of the goddess, and her favors were sought in bringing rain for the crops. Two young girls would carry baskets containing offerings on their heads to a grotto by the temple of Aphrodite. New clothes were made to clothe her statue, and these were led in procession to her temple on a boat with her new cloak as its sail.

It was at Midsummer that the titan Prometheus ("Sun Wheel") brought fire from the heavens as a gift for his creation, humankind.[10] He entered Olympus by stealth and lit a torch from the fiery chariot of the sun, then smuggled the fire to earth secured in a fennel stalk. Like the Irish sun god Lugh, he was a master and teacher of all arts and skills.

In Corinth the goddess of midsummer was golden Aphrodite, the sea-born goddess of love and desire. She was also worshipped in her aspect of Urania, Queen of Heaven.

Africa

The Islamic people of North Africa continue to kindle bonfires on Midsummer Eve, particularly in Morocco and Algeria. The day is sometimes dedicated to Fatima, daughter of Mohammed, and the well-known symbol of the Hand of Fatima is said to relate to the five pillars of Islam, though she is probably a much earlier Pagan goddess in origin.

In Swaziland the summer solstice (here around December 21) marks the start of the new year. When it coincided with the full moon, a ceremony called Incwala was held to strengthen and renew the king. Virgin youths would bring back branches from a magic tree, used to enclose the king's sanctuary. The king would take a magic wand representing fertility and strike a black bull with it, which the youths would then catch and sacrifice. The next day the king would eat green foods representing the new year while his people celebrated by dancing and singing. At sunset the king would dress as an animal and hurl a gourd representing the old year at his warriors. The next day his cheeks are painted white, representing the full moon, and on the final day all the ritual objects used were burned and the king was washed, the falling water representing the coming rains.

Eastern Europe

As elsewhere, the Bulgarian celebration of Midsummer is very ancient, a time when the forces of nature were placated. The Bulgarians said that the sun danced and whirled swords about itself as it rose on Midsummer Day, though it lost its way as it came up and had to be shown the way by the Dawn Maiden. The Bulgarian festival of Midsummer today includes a celebration of the rose-picking season with carnivals, processions, folk songs, and dances.

The Serbians thought that the sun was aware of its mortality and decline on Midsummer Day and this made it hesitate and stop three times, overcome by fear of

winter. In Poland the sun was said to bathe in the river and dance and frolic in the sky. Girls danced clockwise singing to it, encouraging it to play.

Today in Slovenia the summer solstice customs are appropriated to the celebration of independence on June 25. There is music in the streets, food, drink, and fireworks at midnight. However, these midsummer meetings and fairs can be traced back into the remote past. One old custom involved the climbing of mountains and hills.

In Russia the death of the vegetation spirit was celebrated at Midsummer, when the days begin to decline. On Midsummer Eve a figure of Kupalo was made of straw and dressed in women's clothes with a necklace and floral crown. A summer tree decked with ribbons is set up and given the name of Marena ("winter" or "death"). A table is set up nearby with food and drink, and the straw figure of Kupalo placed by it. Then a bonfire is lit and the men and women in couples leap over it, carrying the figure with them. The next day the figure and tree are stripped of their ornaments and thrown into a stream.[11]

In Hungary swineherds would produce a fire on Midsummer Eve by rotating a wheel around a wooden axle wrapped in hemp. They would then drive their pigs through the fire to protect them. In Swabia the "fire of heaven" was kindled by igniting a cartwheel, smeared with pitch and plaited with straw, and fastened on a pole twelve feet high. This was made on the top of a mountain, and the people would recite certain set words.[12]

The Baltic sun goddess was called Saule. Her daughter is the dawn. On Midsummer Eve people stayed up all night in the hope of seeing her dance as she came over the horizon at dawn. They assembled on a hill and raised a bonfire on a pole, and danced and sang around it, sharing a meal of cheese and mead. They bathed in the holy waters, the rivers and streams that flowed east toward the rising sun. This was considered to be both healing and lucky, particularly for anyone looking for a potential marriage partner. The festival was called *Ligo*, meaning "swaying," since the sun is supposed to dance on this day. The hearth fire was allowed to go out and was then relit with much ceremony. At all other times the fire was kept going constantly.[13]

Modern Lithuanian Pagans call the summer solstice festival Rasa.

Spain

In Spain several obvious Pagan customs have become part of the Christian celebrations. In San Pedro Manrique firewalking takes place on St. John's Eve (June 23). Three girls called *Pure Ones* carry baskets of bread on their heads to solicit the blessing of Mary, Queen of Heaven. Horse racing and dancing form part of the celebrations.

The custom of bullfighting is a remnant of ancient rites celebrating the sky god, often represented as a bull, and whose chosen sacrifice was the bull.

The Americas

Midsummer was and is still an important festival in numerous places in North America. In Quebec, Canada, the Feast of St. Jean Baptiste is celebrated with a public holiday, fireworks, feasting, parades, and dancing.

The Natchez Indians in the southern part of the United States worshipped the sun and believed their ruler was descended from him. The Hopi Indians of Arizona would have masked men wearing bright paint and feathers who danced their special rituals. They represented the dancing spirits of rain and fertility called *kachinas*. The kachinas were messengers between humans and the gods. At Midsummer the kachinas leave the Hopi villages to return to their homes in the mountains. While they are there, for half the year, they are believed to visit the dead underground and hold ceremonies for them.

The Chumash Nation of southern California holds a summer solstice gathering every year on Pine Mountain. The peak was once called *Iwihinmu*, which means "place of mystery."

The Feast of St. John

The date of the summer solstice varies between June 19 and 23, while Midsummer is pegged to June 24, which is St. John's Day in the Christian calendar. The Pagan festivities of the solstice were appropriated to the Feast of John the Baptist, the cousin who baptized Jesus and announced that he was the savior foretold by the Hebrew prophets. The baal fires became fires of St. John, whom Jesus called "a burning and shining light."

---

1. This wedding of earth and sky is one of the recurring themes of Midsummer, and we will explore it in greater detail later on.

2. Please note that mistletoe berries are very poisonous.

3. Nigel Pennick, *Runic Astrology* (Wellingborough: Aquarian Press, 1990).

4. Robert Nelson, *Finnish Magic* (Saint Paul, MN: Llewellyn, 1999).

5. J. G. Frazer, *The Golden Bough* (1922: reprint, London: Macmillan, 1957).

6. Lawrence Durdin-Robertson, *The Year of the Goddess* (Wellingborough: Aquarian Press, 1990).

7. Pliny, *Natural History XVIII.*

8. Lawrence Durdin-Robertson, *The Year of the Goddess* (Wellingborough: Aquarian Press, 1990).

9. Robert Graves, *The White Goddess* (London: Faber and Faber, 1961).

10. Prometheus formed humankind from clay and water.

11. J. G. Frazer, *The Golden Bough* (1922: reprint, London: Macmillan, 1957).

12. Ibid.

13. Sheena McGrath, *The Sun Goddess* (London: Blandford, 1997).

Midsummer Customs

There are a number of customs associated with Midsummer, most of which celebrate the light and encourage the power of the sun with sympathetic magic in the form of bonfires, rolling wheels, circle dances, and torchlight processions. Because the energy of the sun infuses the whole of nature, it is a potent time for gathering plants, seeking healing, or practicing divination.

Midsummer Bonfires

Midsummer fires once blazed all across Europe and North Africa. As far east as Siberia, the Buryat tribe jumped over fires to purify and protect themselves. Such ritual fires had the power to protect the revelers from evil spirits, bad fairies, and wicked witches. They also warded off the powers of bane, blight, dark, death, and winter. At one time no self-respecting village would be without its Midsummer fire, while in towns and cities the mayor and corporation actually paid for its construction, and the jollities accompanying it were often very elaborate. Even today some fires are still lit.[1]

The word *bonfire* has an unclear etymology. It may be *boon-fire*, signifying a time of goodwill. It may be from the Nordic *baun,* meaning "torch" or "bane-fire," as it was a fire of purification and dispelled all evil things. It could even be *bone-fire*, since bones were often added. In the thirteenth century it was recorded that in Shropshire there were three types of fire, one of bones only called a *bonfire*, one of wood only called a *wakefire*, and a third of bones and wood called *St. John's Fire*.[2]

The Midsummer fire had particular characteristics. It was constructed in a round shape on a sacred spot near a holy well, on a hilltop, or on a border of some kind. Such liminal sites were sacred to the Celts, who counted any boundary a magical place between places, giving entrance to and from the Otherworld. The fire was lit at sunset on Midsummer Eve, either with needfire kindled by the friction of two pieces of oak, or with a twig of gorse, itself a plant sacred to the sun.

In parts of England it was the convention on St. John's Eve to light large bonfires after sundown to ward off evil spirits. This was known as "setting the watch." A Tudor poem declared:

When midsomer comes, with havens and bromes they do bonefires make,
And swiftly, then, the nimble young men runne leaping over the same.
The women and maydens together do couple their handes.
With bagpipes sounde, they daunce a rounde; no malice among them stands.[3]

Some localities also had a roasted ram feast for the occasion and there were various other customs associated with the event.[4] Men and women danced around the fires and often jumped through them for good luck; to be blackened by the fire was considered very fortuitous indeed. Looking at the flames through larkspur flowers was thought to strengthen the eyesight. A branch lit at the fire was passed over the backs of animals to preserve them from disease. As late as 1900 at least one old farmer in Somerset would pass a burning branch over and under all his horses and cattle.[5] The Cornish even passed children over the flames to protect them from disease in the coming year.

To this day, on June 23 in Carn Brae the first bonfire in a chain across Cornwall is lit.[6] The chain extends from Lands End through to Sennen, Sancread Beacon, Carn Galver, and St. Agnes Beacon to the Tamar River. The local clergyman blesses the bonfires, in Cornish, while herbs and wild flowers are burnt. Young people leap across the embers to drive away evil and to bring good luck. At St. Cleer the fire is crowned with a broomstick, and a sickle with a newly cut oak handle is thrown onto the flames to ensure the fertility of crops and men.

In Ireland large communal fires were lit and there would be music, dancing, and merriment around them. Some were so huge that a ladder was required to set the final fuel on the top. According to Lady Wilde, the young men would strip to the waist and leap backward and forward over the flames a number of times. The one who braved the greatest blaze was considered the victor over the powers of evil and was greeted with applause. When the fires had burned lower, the young girls would jump through, leaping backward and forward three times for luck and a speedy marriage. The married women then walked through the embers of the fire, and finally when the fire was all but burnt out the yearling cattle were led through the warm ashes. A hazel twig would be set alight and drawn over the backs of the animals. These twigs were then considered fertility charms and used thereafter to drive the cattle to and from watering places. Eventually, after singing and storytelling, everyone would take a brand from the fire to their homes to rekindle the hearth fire. This had to be done without dropping the brand or letting it go out, and the men competed to be the first to reach home with a brand, for he brought the luck of the year with him.[7]

Broken rosaries, religious statuettes, and books were thrown into the fire as a pious way of disposing of them. People would parade around the fire saying their rosaries or casting a pebble into the flames at the end of each prayer. The ashes would be taken home to sprinkle on the fields as a fertility charm or given to the old and sick to help ease their passing. The ashes were also used in charms to cure various diseases.

In Scotland the Midsummer fires were frowned on and forbidden by the Protestant Church after the Reformation. However, the inhabitants of northeast Scotland were reluctant to comply, as they believed that fire carried around the fields protected the crops and livestock. After more than a hundred years of struggle, the Church gave up, and the Reverend J. Bisset lit a fire at his own gate and spread a table for the revelers.[8] The fires once again flourished, and wealthy merchants left bequests for them in their wills.

In the Shetlands, where the islanders are of Viking descent, the Johnmas fires were very popular, built with a foundation of bones, straw, seaweed, feathers, wool, and flowers. On the top a little bowl of fish oil was set, and a great blaze ensued. Any broken pots would be thrown onto it. In Orkney the fires were made of heather and peat and burned from sunset to sunrise.

In Germany images of the Winter Witch (the hag goddess of winter) and evil spirits were burned on the Midsummer fire. Images of animals associated with the sun were also burned to give it strength, including cats, cocks, and bulls. The fires were sympathetic magic to encourage the sun to shine enough to provide a good harvest. As people danced around the fires they would wear chaplets of mugwort and vervain. When they came to leave, they would cast the herbs into the fire saying, "May all my ill luck depart and burn with these."[9]

In Sweden the night of St. John was celebrated as the most joyous of the year. Bonfires, called *Baldur's Fires*, were lit at dusk on hilltops and other eminencies. The fires consisted of nine different woods, and fungi were thrown onto the blaze to counteract the power of trolls, for the mountains open at Midsummer and all such fairies and spirits pour forth.

In Brittany the *Tad-You* was a person who oversaw the lighting and burning of the fire, as well as all the prayers and the blessing of the furze used to light the fire. A girl who dances around the Brittany baal fire will be married within the year.

In Wales the fires were lit from nine different types of wood with herbs and sweet-smelling flowers thrown onto them.

On the Celtic Isle of Man the islanders lit Midsummer fires on the windward side of every cornfield, and carried blazing torches over the fields to bless them. The ashes were credited with fertility powers, as were the embers and even the smoke. As in Ireland, these fires were as common as those of Beltane, or more so. This seems to disprove those who claim that the solstice was not celebrated by the Celts, but only in those areas with a Saxon or Nordic influence.

Rolling Wheels

Blazing wheels symbolize the sun rolling through the heavens. The ancient Pagans of Aquitaine rolled a flaming wheel down a hill to a river and then took the charred pieces to the temple of the sky god. Fun customs are hard to kill, and instances of wheel rolling were recorded right into the twentieth century. In the vale of Glamorgan, Wales, people conveyed trusses of straw to the top of a hill. A large cartwheel was swathed with the straw and set alight, and the wheel rolled downhill. If the fire went out before it reached the bottom, this indicated a good harvest.[10] At Buckfastleigh in Devon, a wheel, lit at sunset, was guided with sticks to encourage it to reach a stream. If it did, then this meant good luck for the community.

Torchlight Processions

Torches would be lit at the bonfire and these would be carried inside the milking parlor to keep milk and butter safe from evil magic, and then around the fields and growing crops as a protection and blessing. The torches were afterward attached to the fences and left to burn all night. The ashes of the bonfires were scattered in the corn as an aid to fertility.[11]

In towns, some of these torchlight processions reached lavish proportions. Garland-bedecked bands of people, sometimes called a *marching watch*, carried cressets (lanterns on poles) as they wandered from one bonfire to another. Often morris dancers attended them, with players dressed as unicorns, dragons, and hobbyhorses.

Circle Dancing

It is said that at midnight on Midsummer Eve a person who runs backward seven times around Chanctonbury Ring will conjure up the devil.[12] Running or dancing in circles was an integral part of the worship of the sun god. In this case, as in many others in which circling clockwise around a particular place allegedly raises the "devil," we are speaking of distorted folk memories of sun-god worship.

All sorts of creatures are said to emerge from their lairs to dance in a circle on this night. A group of skeletons emerge from and dance around the roots of an old oak tree at Broadwater Green in Sussex until dawn. Fairy mounds open and the little people come forth to dance to their lovely, unearthly music in the moonlight. But beware: Any human who joins them in their ring will be forced to dance with them forever.

On this night various stone circles of Britain and Ireland are supposed to come alive and dance. This is patently a folk memory of ancient rites concerned with the stones, which are often said to be heathen or irreligious dancers turned to stone.

Divination at Midsummer

Midsummer is a time for magic and divination, when the Sidhe and the spirits are abroad. The twelfth-century Christian mystic Bartholomew Iscanus declared, "He who at the feast of St. John the Baptist does any work of sorcery to seek out the future shall do penance for fifteen days."[13] Young girls would use the magic of the season to divine their future husbands. According to one charm, a girl should circle three times around the church as midnight strikes saying:

Hemp seed I sow,
Hemp seed I hoe,
Hoping that my true love will come after me and mow.

Looking over her shoulder she should see a vision of her lover following her with a scythe. Placing nodules from the root of mugwort under her pillow would enable her to dream of her lover instead. Other less pleasant secrets could also be learned: If you stand in the churchyard on this night, a vision of all those who will die this year will pass before your eyes.

The Midsummer Tree

You might think that the erection of the maypole is a tradition associated exclusively with May Day (Beltane), but you would be wrong. The raising of the Midsummer tree is an authentic Midsummer custom found in many areas, including Wales, England, and Sweden.

The custom was called "raising the birch" (*Codi'r Fedwen*) in south Wales, and "the summer branch" in the north, and the dancing around it "the dance of the birch." In Glamorgan the birch was erected on St. John's Eve and was called *y fedwen haf*, or "summer birch." It was decorated with ribbons, flowers, and even pictures. A weathercock with gilded feathers surmounted it. The cock or rooster was a sacred bird among the Celts, and a bird of the sun. The cry of the cock at sunrise indicates the end of the darkness and the start of the day. Celtic festivals were held from dusk till cock crow of the next morning.

Sometimes one village would try to steal another village's pole, and it was considered very ill fated and a disgrace to lose one in this fashion. The bereft village was not allowed to raise another until they had succeeded in stealing one from elsewhere, and the poles were guarded all night by groups of youths and men. In Carmarthenshire the branches of the summer birch were not trimmed off to make a pole, but were decorated with garlands and wreaths of flowers.

In Sweden and Finland, also, a Midsummer tree of birch was set up and decorated. The villagers danced around it, and lit fires and jumped over them. In Russia the summer tree is decked with ribbons.

Magical Herbs

At Midsummer, foliage and flowering is at its fullest just before fruiting begins. This makes it the ideal time to gather herbs and flowers. An eleventh-century Anglo-Saxon medical text described gathering vervain at Midsummer to cure liver complaints.[14] Other customs included decking the house (especially over the front door) with birch, fennel, St. John's wort, orpine, and white lilies. Even churches were decorated with birch and fennel.

There is a wealth of herb lore associated with the summer solstice, all of it quite revealing when examined in relation to folk memories of more ancient beliefs. Several plants were thought to have particular magical properties on this night, especially vervain and St. John's wort. Indeed, Midsummer Eve in Spain is called the *Night of the Vervain.*

Yellow-flowered St. John's wort, an emblem of the sun, would be gathered on the eve and made into garlands. It was believed to possess the quality of protecting the wearer against all manner of evil. Legend has it that if a young woman should pick St. John's wort on the morning of Midsummer with the dew still fresh upon it, she will marry within a year. Yarrow was also gathered for medicinal purposes and also to be used in marriage divination by young girls. By placing a bit of the herb under the girl's pillow, she would dream of her future husband.

The elder was a Celtic sacred tree, associated with the Crone Goddess, but the Christian Church, in its attempts to denigrate the Old Religion, gave it a bad reputation. It was naturally regarded as a witch and was avoided after dark. Falling asleep beneath it put one in the power of witches. It is said that if you cut an elder tree on Midsummer Eve it will bleed real blood.

Vigils

It was the custom for people to watch the sun go down on St. John's Eve, then to stay awake for the entire length of the short night and watch the sun come up again. In the sixteenth century, John Stow of London described it is a time when people set out tables of food and

drink, which they invited their neighbors to share, and then made up their quarrels, lit bonfires, and hung their houses with herbs and small lamps.[15]

In Celtic tradition it is one of those times when a would-be bard might seek a lonely spot to await inspiration. There are mountains in Wales where it is said that anyone spending the night there will come down in the morning either mad or a poet.

Anyone watching the sunrise and sunset may be rewarded by a magical or unusual sight such as the one that crowds witness every year at Leek, in Staffordshire, England. They gather at the Parish Church of Edward the Confessor. From the northeast corner of the churchyard, the sun sinks behind Cloud End Hill only to reappear further north a few seconds later and set for a second time.[16]

Water and Wells

On Midsummer Day in Sweden women and girls went to bathe in a river. In Russia women bathed in the river, dipping in it a figure, supposedly of St. John, made from grass and herbs. These acts are sympathetic charms for bringing the life-giving summer rain to nourish the crops.

In Britain it was the custom to visit holy wells just before sunrise on Midsummer Day. The well should be approached from the east and walked around sunwise three times. Offerings such as pins or coins were thrown into the well and its water drunk from a special vessel. One such well was Willie's Muir in Scotland, visited by childless women on Midsummer Eve. An old woman, the human guardian of the well, supervised them as they processed about the spring and splashed their breasts and bottoms with water.[17]

Wells were thought to have guardian spirits or water nymphs living in them. Sometimes these appeared in the form of a fish, a frog, a mermaid, a winged serpent, or even a fly. The practice of making offerings at holy wells dates back to the Bronze Age, or possibly earlier. The Celts and other tribes also sacrificed treasure to lake and river spirits. At the site of Flag Fen in Cambridgeshire, England, over three hundred bronze artifacts were found, including pins and ornaments, rings, and a large number of weapons, including swords and daggers and tools such as chisels and awls.[18]

Stones

An image many people associate with Midsummer is that of modern druids practicing their rites at Stonehenge. It is not known whether the ancient druids used this Neolithic temple of the sun, but its power remains intact today, even when surrounded by fences and tourists.

Stonehenge has been described as an astronomical observatory. It is orientated to the sun at the summer solstice, which rises above the heel stone. Some say this should be "heal stone," as the circle was associated with healing at Midsummer. In the twelfth century, Geoffrey on Monmouth recorded that the stones were washed and the water poured into baths to bathe the sick. The practice continued until the eighteenth century. Others say that the word *heel* may be derived from Helios, Greek god of the sun.

Of course, Stonehenge is not the only circle or site orientated to the summer solstice. Others include Avebury, Stanton Drew, Randwick Barrow, Addington Barrow, Bryn Celli Dhu Temple, Mayburgh Henge, Temple Wood Circles, and Newgrange (which also has midwinter alignments).[19] Other circles have Midsummer legends. As we have seen, some come alive and dance. According to legend, the Rollright Stones' King Stone is a real king turned into stone by a witch. On Midsummer Eve he is said to turn his head, and for hundreds of years pilgrims would visit the circle to witness it. Nearby is a group of stones known as the Whispering Knights, and on Midsummer Eve they will whisper your future, especially that portion concerning your love life.

Morris Men

The folk dancers known as *morris men* are associated with the festival. In Gwent a troupe of morris dancers would all dress in white, apart from the Fool and the *Cadi*, who carried the "summer branch," which was decorated with silver ornaments (watches, spoons, etc., borrowed from the whole village). The Cadi was the master of ceremonies, dressed partly in male clothes and partly in female clothes, with a blackened or masked face and red-rimmed eyes. Including the garland bearer, the party of dancers numbered thirteen—the number of lunar months in the year.

In England the town watch would sometimes be turned out to keep order at large fires. They would be dressed up in fancy costumes and carry cressets of fire—pails of fire hung from poles. They would form a procession, accompanied by morris men, model giants, and pageants, all carrying torches. It must have been a fantastic sight.

It is claimed that morris men date back to Pagan fertility dancers, though the earliest written records are from the thirteenth century. Their costumes are decorated with flowers, ribbons, and bells.

---

1. Though in some cases the practice lapsed and was revived.
2. T. Erbe, ed., *Mirk's Festival* (Early English Text Society, 1905).
3. A. Clark, ed., *The Shires Ballads,* "The Mery Life of the Countriman" (Oxford, 1907), lines 1585–1603.
4. The ram is an ancient symbol of the sun.
5. R. L. Tongue, *Somerset Folklore* (Folklore Society, 1965).
6. Cornwall is a Celtic county in the southwest of England.
7. Lady Wilde, *Ancient Legends, Mystic Charms and Superstitions of Ireland* (London: Ward and Downey, 1878).
8. Marion MacNeill, *The Silver Bough* (Maclellan, 1957).
9. James Frazer, *The Golden Bough* (1922: reprint, London: Macmillan, 1957).
10. Marie Trevelyan, *Folk Lore and Folk Stories of Wales* (1909).
11. This has a scientific basis—wood ash provides a high potash feed for plants.
12. Chanctonbury Ring is a clump of trees on a hilltop earthwork in Sussex, England.
13. J. T. McNeill & H. M. Garner, eds., *Mediaeval Handbooks of Penance* (New York, 1938).
14. G. Storm, *Anglo-Saxon Magic* (1948).
15. C. L. Kingsford, ed., *A Survey of London* (Oxford, 1908).
16. Q. Cooper & P. Sullivan, *Maypoles, Matyrs and Mayhem* (London: Bloomsbury, 1994).
17. F. Marian McNeill, *The Silver Bough* (Edinburgh: Cognate Classics).
18. Marion K. Pearce, "Flag Fen Lake Village," *Silver Wheel* (February 1997).
19. Terence Meaden, *Stonehenge: The Secret of the Solstice* (London: Souvenir Press, Ltd., 1997).

Ancient Themes
for Modern Pagans

Today's Pagans celebrate Midsummer with as much joy as their fore-bears. It is one of the eight major festivals of the Pagan year (the others being the winter solstice, the spring and autumn equinoxes, Imbolc, Beltane, Lammas, and Samhain or Halloween). These festivals celebrate the ebb and flow of energies in the natural world, with each festival having its own themes, traditions, and powers. The energies of Midsummer are concerned with light, fertility, consummation, conception, vitality, healing, and love (as opposed, for example, to Samhain, when the energies are about winding down, death, decay, winter, and endings). This ebb and flow of the Wheel needs to be taken into account when planning activities for festivals.

A Lesser Sabbat?

The feast of the summer solstice, along with the other solar festivals, is often referred to as a Lesser Sabbat, as opposed to the four "fire festivals," or cross-quarter festivals, of Imbolc, Beltane, Lughnasa, and Samhain. This is a misnomer in many ways. For example, Lughnasa was never a fire festival, while both the solstices were.

The controversy in Craft circles dates back to the 1950s and Gerald Gardner, the father of modern Wicca. His own coven allegedly only celebrated the four cross-quarter festivals.[1] Gardner put forward the idea, which had some currency in scholastic circles at the time, that the solstices and equinoxes were a later import from the Middle East. However, there is a great deal of evidence to the contrary.

We have seen that the festival is celebrated around the world. We know that the builders of the megaliths celebrated the solstices and equinoxes. We know that the Saxons and Norsemen held the summer solstice to be a festival of major importance; in northern Europe it was generally considered to be the most important festival of the whole year.[2] Academics are also now challenging the view that the observation of the summer solstice spread from there into Celtic areas.[3] I often read that the Celts did not celebrate the summer solstice, or if they did then the bonfire customs were transferred to it from Beltane. In fact, the reverse is probably true. Midsummer is a far more ancient festival, practiced throughout Britain, Ireland, and Europe prior to the invasion of the Celts, as evidenced by the megalithic sites orientated to the summer solstice. The native people intermarried with the invaders, and were not completely wiped out by them, as some writers seem to assume; genetic testing of Neolithic burials has revealed descendants still living in the same areas. It seems likely that the Celtic "invasion" may have been more a case of the transmission of Celtic culture than a physical invasion in some places. It is inconceivable that the indigenous people would not continue to celebrate their most important festivals—the solstices and equinoxes.

Scholars agree that the Celts absorbed much from the peoples they invaded, and the evidence is plain that the druids considered Midsummer an important festival. In fact, the solstice customs of Celtic Wales, Scotland, Cornwall, and Brittany are perhaps even more enthusiastic than those of nearby Saxon and Viking areas. The wealth of solstice customs in the Celtic lands of Ireland and the Isle of Man also demonstrate the importance of Midsummer in these areas. The nature of these customs indicates their antiquity, and many of them are peculiar to Midsummer, so the theory that they are transposed from Beltane is called into grave question.

Gerald Gardner changed and "improved" much of what he learned at the New Forest Coven. Despite the eightfold nature of the traditional witch's year, he decided that the solstices and equinoxes were later additions to the Craft calendar. He was wrong about this, too. The greatest festival in the year of the old French witches was St. John's Eve.

Most modern-day Pagans, witches, and druids celebrate the festival in some form. Present-day druids know it as Alban Heruin, meaning "light on the shore," referring to the three rays of *awen* representing inspiration, seen as light over the water. Celtic Pagans sometimes call the festival Coamhain, a corruption of the Gaelic *coimhéad* meaning to guard, watch, or observe, referring to the night-long vigil. It is possible that the Saxons called the festival *Litha*, and many Pagans, especially in the United States, know it by this name.

The Problem of the Date

While the solstice generally falls around June 21,[4] Midsummer Eve is fixed as June 23, St. John's Eve, and Midsummer Day as St. John's Day, June 24. Then again, you may read of Old Midsummer Eve and Old Midsummer Day in early July. What on earth is going on? Which is the correct day to hold your festivities?

It is generally accepted that the Christian missionaries persuaded the old Pagans to move their celebrations of the summer solstice to the Feast of St. John the Baptist on June 24, thus pegging a moveable solstice feast to a definite date. However, it is noticeable that while most parts of Europe celebrate on St. John's Day, a significant number of individual areas celebrate on St. Peter and St. Paul's Day, June 28.

At least part of the confusion results from changes made to the calendar. In 1582 Pope Gregory XIII wiped out ten days from the old Julian calendar to make it astronomically correct. However, the Gregorian calendar was not adopted in Britain until 1752 and in Ireland until 1782, by which time eleven days had to be dropped. Some towns refused to move their holiday, and Whalton in Northumberland still lights its fires on Old Midsummer Eve, July 5. From the evidence it seems that the Midsummer festival was a general holiday held over several days around the solstice.

The solstice marks the height of the sun's power. For many this is the day to hallow, and to observe it a few days later would be like celebrating the full moon a few days later than when it actually falls—when the energies are quite different and actually waning. For others, June 23 and 24 have accrued such magic about them over the centuries that these are deemed the correct days to hold the festival. Only you know what feels right for you, and you should work on the day that seems most magical.

Midsummer or the Start of Summer?

On modern calendars in the United States, June 24 is reckoned as the start of summer, not Midsummer, which is a bit confusing and needs some clarification. While it is the start of summer in far-northern countries such as in Scandinavia where summer comes late, it really is Midsummer in Britain, Ireland, and northern/mid-Europe. Summer starts at Beltane (May 1) according to the old Celts.

The summer solstice is the midpoint of the light half of the year reckoned from equinox to equinox. At the vernal equinox day and night are of equal length, but the light is gaining. At the summer solstice it reaches its zenith, then at the autumn equinox day and night are once again of equal length, but the dark is gaining.

Midsummer and the Wheel of the Year

The Craft year of eight festivals is often represented as an eight-spoked wheel. The turning of this wheel symbolizes the turning of the year through the seasons, and each of the eight spokes represents a festival. In the past it was the custom to wrap a wheel in flammable material, light it, and set it rolling down a hill at Midsummer to exemplify the moving forward of the year.

While the Goddess remains constant at the hub of the wheel, the eight festivals mark the phases of the God in his aspects of Vegetation Lord and Sun God. At the midwinter solstice he is born as a babe from the Goddess (the sun born from between the horns of the moon). At Imbolc the Goddess is purified and renewed as a Virgin (the face of the earth is washed by winter rains). At the vernal equinox the young vegetation God emerges and meets the young Goddess (the earth begins to green in spring). At Beltane they marry and the earth flowers. The summer solstice marks the height of the God's powers with the longest day and the fertilization of the Flower Bride; the flowers are pollinated, ready to fruit. At Lughnasa (August 1) we mark the strength of the God as Corn Lord, and the harvest of first fruits. At the autumn equinox day and night are of equal length but the dark is gaining. The grain is harvested and we commemorate the death of the Corn Lord. By Samhain the Vegetation Lord lies in the underworld, the womb of the Goddess, which he rules as king of the dead.

Though the summer solstice marks the zenith of the sun and day of longest light, it is also a day of sadness, because from this day on the light begins to decline, the days shorten, and though this is midsummer we are moving inevitably toward winter.

The Battle of Light and Dark

In the Craft the solar year is often seen as being ruled over by two opposing kings. The Oak King rules the waxing year from midwinter solstice to summer solstice, the part of the year when the hours of daylight increase. The Holly King rules the waning year from summer solstice to winter solstice when the hours of daylight decrease. At each solstice they battle for the hand of the Goddess and the honor of ruling the land. The summer solstice begins with the Oak King in power, but this is relinquished to the Holly King at the close of the festival.

This idea of two gods, one of summer/light and one of winter/darkness, occurred in many myth systems. These two lords, often twins or even hero and dragon/snake, fight for rulership at the beginning of summer and at the beginning of winter.[5] The Greek sun god Apollo killed the python at Delphi with his sun-ray arrows. The serpent represented the powers of darkness, underworld, and earth womb as opposed to Apollo's gifts of light and sky. The Egyptian god Ra, as the solar cat, fought the serpent of darkness Zet, or Set. Similar stories are of sky gods fighting serpents, such as Marduk and Tiamat, Zeus and Typhon, and Yahweh and Leviathan. In Irish myth the Fir Bolgs and Tuatha dé Danaan first fought at Midsummer. The monstrous Fir Bolgs represent the powers of winter, decline, and death.

The dark twin, or the dragon, is not an evil power but merely the other side of the coin. One is light, the other dark, one summer, one winter, one sky, and the other the underworld. Pagans accept these polarities as a necessary part of the whole—winter comes but summer will return. The sun sets, travels through the underworld at night, and is reborn with the dawn. The king dies, returns to the underworld womb of the earth goddess, and is reborn.

In Christian times the theme of these myths were changed and the hero killed the dragon instead of just defeating him for the summer months. According to the Pagan worldview, the slain lord will rise again every year, and the light and dark rule in balance. Later myths see death as a final ending and the light and dark as being in opposition. The gods of the light half of the year became dragon-slaying saints such as St. George and St. Michael, and the dragons they slew became a metaphor for defeated Pagans. The dark became evil, and the fruitful underworld womb of the Goddess became the Christian Hell.

Pagan Midsummer festivities were transferred to the Christian Feast of St. John the Baptist. However, St. John may not be as 100 percent Christian as he seems at first glance. Robert Graves points out that while

the winter solstice celebrates the birth of Jesus, the summer solstice celebrates the birth of John, the elder cousin. This relates them directly to all the ancient twin deities of light and dark, summer and winter.[6] If John is the Oak King of midsummer, Jesus is the Holly King of midwinter—*"Of all the trees that are in the wood, the holly bears the crown,"* as the old Pagan carol says.

Some of the representations of St. John are rather strange for a Christian saint. He is often depicted with horns, furry legs, and cloven hooves like a satyr or woodwose, a wild man of the woods. His shrines, too, are often of a rustic nature, ostensibly because St. John was fond of wandering in the wilderness. It is possible that St. John not only took a Pagan midsummer festival for his feast day, but also the attributes and shrines of an earlier green god. Frazer speculates that he took on the mantle of Tammuz/Adonis, the vegetation god who was honored at Midsummer.

In the Craft today the theme of the battle of light and darkness is usually enacted as a ritual drama with a choreographed battle between the Oak King and the Holly King.

Now is the time of brightness, long days, and warmth. There is the promise of the harvest growing in fields and gardens. The earth is pregnant with goodness, made fertile by the light of the sun. The sun god is in his glory: strong, virile, the husband and lover of the Goddess. The power of the sun on this day is protective, healing, empowering, revitalizing, and inspiring. It imbues a powerful, magical charge into spells, crystals, and herbs. It is a time for fun and joy, for enjoying the light and warmth. Modern Pagans often celebrate Midsummer outdoors and follow the festival with a picnic or barbecue.

Fire Magic

Bonfires and torchlight processions about the fields mark this time of year. This is the season when the sun is at its greatest peak, but begins to decline. It was therefore natural for people to want to protect themselves, their crops, and animals from the powers of decay, winter, and blight that are an inevitable consequence of the decrease of the sun's warmth and vigor. Fire, the "little brother" of the sun, naturally gains greater power when the force of the sun is at its peak.

The sacredness of the Midsummer fire is truly ancient. It is associated with oak wood, with sky and thunder gods, and with fertility. The most venerated type of fire was one that came from the heavens itself, in the form of lightning, St. Elmo's fire; or wild-fire and elf-fire, which are made by projecting the sun's rays through a lens. Otherwise, rubbing two sticks together made the holy fire. At least one of these sticks is always oak, though the other may be of a wood representing the feminine to the oak's masculine. The bonfires also contained oak wood.

It can be argued that the Midsummer fires are the funeral pyres of the summer sun. The Celts thought that there were two sun deities, the summer sun and the winter sun. In *The Golden Bough,* James Frazer speculates that the sacred Oak King was sacrificed on Midsummer Day by being burned alive, after which he was taken to Caer Arianrhod, the whirling, spiral castle located in the Corona Borealis.[7] The solar hero Herakles asked that his Midsummer funeral pyre be on the highest peak and consist of oak and male olive branches.

The customs of Midsummer indicate a ritual ending and new beginning. At the Baltic Midsummer festival, all the hearth fires, which were otherwise never extinguished, were allowed to go out. They were relit with ceremony from a bonfire made on a high hill or a riverbank by rubbing together a stick of oak (male) and one of linden (female). A similar practice was carried out in Ireland. Medieval

witches burned an oak log in the hearth on Midsummer Eve and kept the fire going for a year, after which the ashes were removed to make way for a new log. The ashes were mixed with seed corn and scattered on the earth.

People leaped the fires to cleanse themselves. Fire is the natural element of purification and protection, burning away corruption and consuming decay. The magic of fire is said to break all evil spells. In Ireland a threatened child, cow, woman, house, or man was placed in a protective ring of fire.[8] Candles or embers were carried around women in childbed and around babies before they were named to protect them from the attentions of fairy kidnappers.[9]

Fire plays an important part in Craft rituals. When space and regulations permit, a bonfire is lit outdoors. This fire is used to dispose of any outworn or broken Craft tools and books. When the flames have died down a little, it is leapt over for protection and luck. When space does not permit, three yellow or gold candles are lit in the cauldron. Again, the cauldron is jumped over for fertility and good fortune. A torch or candle lantern is carried around property or crops to ensure their preservation and fruitfulness.[10] Fireworks can be a lovely part of the celebration, particularly catherine wheels, a good modern substitution for the fiery wheels that were once rolled down hillsides to represent the sun.

Healing Water

While Midsummer is a sun and fire festival, it is also a festival of water. In bygone days people would make pilgrimages to holy wells at Midsummer to solicit cures or to make offerings of coins, pins, and flowers to the resident deity.

Wells and springs issue from the earth womb of the life-giving Goddess. Along with caves and clefts, they were regarded as entrances to this womb, which all life springs from and returns to at death. Entering a cave was akin to entering the womb of the earth. In Sumerian, *matu* meant "womb," "under-world," and "cave."[11] The word comes from a root word for *mother*, rendering the Latin *mater*, the Teutonic *modar*, and the English *mother*. All such places were held as sacred to the Goddess.

With the coming of Christianity, these wells were taken over by the Church and said to be sacred to certain saints. In Ireland they are often dedicated to St. Brigid, who was originally the Pagan goddess Brighid. In Britain they are more likely to be hallowed to St. Ann, once the Pagan goddess Anna, Annis, or Anu.

Midsummer is the festival of Sul Minerva, the goddess of the famous healing springs at Aqua Sulis, or modern-day Bath, in the south of England. It is at this season that the various well-dressing rituals of England begin and continue throughout the summer. Though these now come under the auspices of the Christian Church, they are very ancient and Pagan in origin and are designed to honor the spirit of the water. The wells are dressed with elaborate pictures made of flowers.

Water becomes very important at the height of summer when the growing crops need irrigating.

Thunder Gods, Oak Trees, and Druids

This is also the season of necessary rain and the time of thunderstorms. While rain is always life-giving, the thunderstorms that occur in the sultry midsummer heat demonstrate the presence of the virile sky god, roaring like a bull and flashing his lightning ax. It is his semen—the rain—that fertilizes the earth goddess. In some myth systems it is the thunder god who is her mate, not the sun. Aeschylus declared:

> *The holy Heaven doth live to wed the ground,*
> *And Earth conceives a love of marriage,*
> *The rain that falls from husband Heaven*
> *Impregnates Earth; and she for mortal men gives birth*
> *To pastoral herbage and Ceres' corn.*[12]

Thunder gods are invariably associated with the oak tree because the oak attracts more lightning than any other tree. Thus the power of the god is mediated from the sky, through the earth realm (the tree) into the underworld via its roots. These

oaks were venerated as the dwelling place of the god. Into the twentieth century, any oak that was struck be lightning was considered particularly powerful, and people would often travel for miles to take a small piece of such a tree to be used as a talisman.

The best known of all the sacred groves of Greece was Dodona in Epirus, sacred to Zeus, the Greek sky/thunder god. It is said that thunderstorms rage more frequently there than anywhere else in Europe, and this is probably why the temple was established there. Bronze gongs were hung on the trees, and as the wind swayed them they were meant to imitate thunder. The oak was also sacred to Thor, the Norse thunder god. His well-known symbol of the hammer is in fact thunder. Boniface felled an oak in which he was believed to reside during the conversion of the Germans. Oaks figured in many representations of Taranis, the British thunder god. The Finnish god of thunder was Ukko ("Oak"), and Rauni ("Rowan") was his wife. In Russia the oak god was called *Perun*, his name meaning "thunderbolt." The Canaanite storm god Baal was depicted with an ax and pointed cap.

The Lithuanian god of the oak was Perkaunas, or Perunu ("Thunder"), Lord of the Universe, the supreme god or creator god, depicted with a hammer or ax. If lightning struck a tree, rock, or person, they were believed to hold some of his sacred fire. Eternal fires of oak wood were burned in his honor. If they were extinguished, they could only be rekindled by rubbing oak sticks together. At Midsummer his lightning strikes the oak, causing its blood to fertilize the earth:

When the morning star was wedded
Perkunas rode through the doorway
And a green oak was shattered.
Then forth the oak's blood spurted
Besprinkling all my garments,
Besprinkling, too, my crownlet.[13]

The oak is the king of the forest, huge, living for centuries. In Britain there are reputed to be oaks that have stood for a thousand years. Most of them have decayed and have hollow centers. The roots of the oak are said to extend as far underground as its branches do above, making a perfect symbol for a god whose powers royally extend to the heavens, middle earth, and the underworld equally. It is a symbol of the law "As above, so below."

The Roman writer Pliny recognized that the Greek word *drus*, meaning "oak," is related to the Celtic word *druid*. Some authors suggest the second syllable may be commensurate with the Indo-European *wid*, meaning "know," and the derived meaning would be "oak knowledge."[14] It has been suggested that *bard* may be formed from the word *barr*, meaning "branch," as *bard* in Welsh is *bardd*.

The Celts carved god statues from oak boughs, which were kept in the sacred grove of oaks where there were also sacred springs and holy wells. When the oak flowered, around the time of the midsummer solstice, the druids made an infusion from the flower buds as an internal cleanser for the body, and washed in water found in the hollows of oak as a ritual cleanser for the Midsummer rites.

In England many old oaks are still known as "bull oaks." The storm god is also associated with the bull. The ancient Mesopotamian storm god was depicted with a bull's horns, tail, and spiraling hair. Baal has spiraled hair, reminiscent of a bull's pelt. He took the form of a bull to mate with his sister in the form of a cow. The druids thought that the sky bull mated with the earth cow at Midsummer. The bull is one of the most powerful European animals, synonymous with strength and virility. His roar and the crash of his hooves mimic the thunder of the sky god. In Asia and Europe, from the Neolithic age onward, the bull and the ax or hammer were associated with the thunder/sky god. The bull was his chosen sacrifice, and and remnants of this custom survive to this day in the bullfights of Spain.

Midsummer Poles and the Flower Bride

In Scandinavia, the British Isles, and Eastern Europe, Midsummer trees were cut and decorated with ribbons and flowers. These cut and decorated poles represent the vitality of the vegetative life force in spring and summer and are made from deciduous birch.[15] They represent the phallic, fertilizing power of the God, thrust into the womb of the Earth Mother. Such trees formed part of druidic activities; there are various illustrations of Celtic rituals including a pole thrust into a well or earth cavity, regarded as entrances to the womb of Mother Earth.

The tree or pole also functions as an *axis mundi*, joining the worlds of gods and humankind in the ritual cycle. Around them, sunwise and antisunwise, dances take place, winding down one season and winding up another.

Such poles, called *maypoles*, also form part of the Beltane (May Day) festivities. However, while Beltane commemorates the marriage of the God and Goddess, Midsummer marks the impregnation or fertilization of the Goddess as Flower Bride. Craft tradition venerates this as the time of flower opening when foliage

and flowers are at their fullest before fruiting begins. Bees and insects are busy pollinating blossoms. The season is sacred to Blodeuwedd, the Welsh flower bride of the sun god Llew. Her name means "Flower Face," and she was created by two of Llew's magicians when his mother, Arianrhod, forbade him to marry a human woman. Eventually Blodeuwedd was unfaithful to him with Gronw Pebyr ("Strong Young Man") and caused his death. As a punishment she was changed into an owl. Though some see her as the archetypal rebellious woman,[16]

she is in fact the blossoming earth goddess in the summer, and her two lovers are summer and winter, or the gods of the waxing and waning sun. A similar story is told of Guinevere, Arthur's queen. Her name means "white phantom," associating her, like Blodeuwedd, with the owl. She is also called the *Flower Bride* and was stolen away by King Melwas of the Summer Country and rescued by Arthur, another sun god. In a later story she betrays Arthur with Lancelot of the Lake. Both she and Blodeuwedd are sovereign goddesses of the land whom the king/seasonal god must marry in order to rule.

Flowers play a great part in the Midsummer festivities. They are made into wreaths and garlands, cast into the fires, and thrown into holy wells and springs. In many parts of the world a rose festival takes place in June. Roses and rosettes are emblems of the sun, like other flowers with rayed petals, but also represent the vulva of the Goddess. Roses are sacred to the goddess of love, and legend has it that they sprang from the blood of Venus, whose rites are celebrated at this time. Couples at weddings in ancient Rome wore chaplets of roses. Because this is the season of fertilization, blossoming, and verdant life, it was the preferred time for betrothals and weddings. June is still the favorite month for marriages, and is named after the Roman goddess Juno, patroness of women and marriage.

St. John's Eve is traditionally the time for declaring love, as in an old Sardinian folk custom. A few months previously a boy will have asked a girl to become his sweetheart, and having accepted she plants a pot with some grain and nurtures it until Midsummer Eve. Together with friends and relatives they process to the church and break the pot by throwing it at the door. Afterward they feast, dance in circles, and sing a song called "Sweethearts of St. John."

In other areas the pots were placed on the windowsill with a priapic figure made of paste, and decorated with ribbons. A bonfire was kindled in the public square and people danced and made merry around it. Girls and boys who wished to become "sweethearts of St. John" had to pass a stick through the flames to each other three times.

In Sicily boys and girls become "sweethearts of St. John" by performing ceremonies over hairs drawn from their heads, then tying them together and throwing them in the air. In some villages sweethearts present each other with sprouting corn, lentils, and seed, planted forty days before the festival. These potted plants are a relic of the ancient gardens of Adonis, sown during the heat of midsummer in honor of the vegetation god. Their rapid growth and withering ritually imitate his growth and harvest sacrifice.

Herb Craft

On Midsummer morning the druids ventured out to collect herbs. Herbs are part of the bounty of the sun god, who is always a patron of healing and medicine. The Greek sun god Apollo was the father of the god of medicine Asklepios. The Celtic sun god Belinos was a patron of healing and renewal.

In Irish tradition the physician of the gods was Dian Cécht. His son Miach and daughter Airmid were trained to follow in their father's footsteps, and it was they who fashioned a new arm made from silver for Nuada after he lost his own in the battle with the Formorians.[17] Their cleverness made Dian Cécht insanely envious of their talents, which far surpassed his own. In a rage he beat his son about the head with a sword until he was dead. Miach was buried, and from his grave 365 herbs sprang up, each for a separate part of the body. Airmid picked them and carefully laid them out in order on her mantle, according to the properties of each. However, Dian Cécht overturned the mantle, the herbs were scattered, and humankind lost the power of the herbs to heal every disease that afflicts us. The knowledge of only a few remained. Breton herbalists retain something of this tradition, but only know twenty-six herbs that relate to parts of the body. Of these vervain is the head, St. John's wort the blood, and mugwort the waist.[18]

Craft herbalists use herbs for a variety of purposes. The first is to heal, the second for spiritual inspiration (the use of herbs in teas and wines, incense, and magical oils), the third in spells, and the fourth in divination.

Every self-respecting witch takes the opportunity afforded by the magic of Midsummer to collect a good supply of herbs to preserve for use throughout the year. At the end of this time any herbs left over from the previous year should be thrown onto the Midsummer bonfire.

The Marriage of Heaven and Earth

This is the time when the earth goddess is fertilized by the life-giving rain, or by the lightning flash of the thunder god. As we have seen, the Midsummer tree thrust into the earth symbolizes this. However, another form of this sacred marriage takes place at the summer solstice, one perhaps more ancient still. This is the marriage of the sun and earth, of sky father and earth mother, that makes the earth fruitful.

At the midsummer solstice Neolithic people would gather outside Stonehenge to witness this *hieros gamos*. As the sun rises behind the heel stone, a phallic shadow is cast into the circle and touches the so-called "altar" stone, consummating the marriage.[19] The circle is an ancient symbol of the Goddess or her womb, and any stone with a hole in it represents the Goddess, including stone circles. The phallic heel stone stands outside the henge and for only a few days around the summer solstice does its shadow touch the altar stone (itself a lozenge shape, another ancient goddess vulva symbol). Terence Meaden speculates that this stone is an axis mundi, linking the earth plane to the realms of the gods. The phallic shadow can only enter

through the middle triathlon, another threefold symbol of the goddess. The circle constitutes a bounded space where gods and humankind can interact.

In the Craft, the fertilization of the Goddess by the God takes place when the wand is plunged into the cauldron, representing the womb of the Goddess, with these words:

The knife to the cup, the rod to the cauldron,
the sun to the earth, but the flesh to the spirit.

Gods and Goddesses of Midsummer

Midsummer is the time when flowers open, and it is sacred to flower maidens such as Blodeuwedd, Guinevere, Flora, Rosea, Xochiquetzal, and Chasca, and to earth goddesses like Anat, Erce, Gaia, and Tellus Mater. The fertile womb of the Goddess is ripe, and the rites of Cerridwen, goddess of the cauldron, and Hebe, the cup-bearer, also take place at this time.

The summer solstice is the highest point of the year ruled over by queens of heaven such as Juno, Hera, Frigga, Amaunet, Inanna, Ishtar, and Urania. In some traditions it is the time when the twin gods of light and dark battle for the hand of the sovereign goddess Danu, Anu, Macha, Epona, Guinevere, or Rhiannon.

Of course, Midsummer is also sacred to sun gods such as Amun Ra, Arthur, Apollo, Baldur, Bel, Belinos, Bochica, Helios, Hu, Hyperion, Lleu Llaw Gyffes, Lugh, Marduk, Mithras, Perun, Pushan, Ra, Shamash, Surya, Tezcatlipoca, Tonatiuh, Upulero, Uttu, and Vishnu. In some traditions, including some Celtic ones, the deity of the sun is female. Sun goddesses include Amaterasu, Arinna, Barbale, Barbet, Bast, Grian, Iarila, Knowee, Saule, Sol, Solntse, Sunna, and Yhi.

Midsummer thunder gods such as Baal, Donar, Hadad, Indra, Janicot, Jupiter, Nyame, Shango, Tranis, Thor, Thinar, Tlaloc, Ukko, and Zeus bring the fertilizing rain.

Other deities that are honored at this time include fire gods and goddesses like Arani, Brighid, Aine, Goibniu, Govannon, Hestia, and Vesta, and love goddesses such as Aphrodite, Astarte, Erzulie, Freya, and Hathor. Midsummer is accounted the hinge of the year and the festival of liminal deities such as Syn, Cardea, and Janus. (For more information on Midsummer gods and goddesses, see appendix 4.)

Applying Midsummer Themes
in Your Own Magical Life

We have explored the themes of Midsummer, and in your Midsummer celebrations you should try to include some of the following:

- Outdoor celebrations with coven/family/friends
- Circle dancing
- Merrymaking
- Feasting
- Fires
- Torchlight processions
- Witnessing the rising and zenith of the sun
- Bathing in healing waters
- Ritual enactment of the fertilization of the Flower Bride
- Ritual enactment of the marriage of heaven and earth
- Acknowledgment of the seasonal triumph of vegetation
- The battle of light and dark, Oak King and Holly King
- It is the traditional time for weddings and handfastings, should any couple wish to marry
- Love magic
- Divination
- Herb magic

The following chapters will give you some ideas on each of these.

Midsummer on a Personal Level

The sun represents both the daylight world and the Inner Light. While the moon rules the night and the unconscious, the sun rules the day and the conscious. On a personal level, Midsummer is time to celebrate your achievements, to acknowledge your own talents and your power of acting in the outer world. It is a time for fun and joy, for relishing the light and warmth.

1. Michael Howard, "High Days and Holidays," *Deosil Dance* (Imbolc, 1994).
2. Ronald Hutton, *The Stations of the Sun* (Oxford University Press, 1996).
3. Ibid.
4. It can vary between June 19 and 23.
5. In some cases the solstices, in others the equinoxes, and in others still Beltane and Samhain.
6. Robert Graves, *The White Goddess* (London: Faber and Faber, 1965).
7. James Frazer, *The Golden Bough* (1922: reprint, London: Macmillan, 1957).
8. Lady Wilde, *Ancient Legends, Mystic Charms and Superstitions of Ireland* (London, 1878).
9. Ibid.
10. If you like, you can just light a candle and carry it around your home or bedroom.
11. Terence Meaden, *Stonehenge: The Secret of the Solstice* (London: Souvenir Press, 1997).
12. Aeschylus (Greek poet, 525–456 B.C.E.), *Tragicorum Graecorum*.
13. Traditional folk song.
14. John King, *The Celtic Druids' Year* (London: Blandford, 1995).
15. As a counterpoint to the Midwinter or Yule tree, which is made from an evergreen and represents the survival of the vegetation spirit, even in barren winter.
16. Like Eve, created from the rib of Adam.
17. From the Gaelic *Fomhoiré,* "Sea Giants." These hideous monsters were the original inhabitants of Ireland. The people of Nemed had to pay the Formorians a tribute of two of their children and some cattle every November. They represent the spirits of winter, death, and disease.
18. Alexei Kondratiev, *Celtic Rituals* (New Celtic Publishing, 1999).
19. Terence Meaden, *Stonehenge: The Secret of the Solstice* (London: Souvenir Press, 1997).

Midsummer Magic and Divination

"The young maid stole through the cottage door,
And blushed as she sought the Plant of pow'r—
Thou silver glow-worm, O lend me thy light,
I must gather the mystic St. John's wort tonight,
The wonderful herb, whose leaf will decide
If the coming year shall make me a bride."
—Old poem

As we have already seen, Midsummer is a day of potent magic, a time when the Otherworld is near and it is possible to see into the future. A wide variety of divination techniques were, and in some cases still are, employed by country people. Farmers view the weather on the solstice as an indicator of the bounty of the harvest: if it rains today it indicates a poor, wet grain harvest, but a large crop of apples and pears.

Love Divination

In bygone days young girls would take the opportunity to perform various acts of divination, usually to discover whom they would marry. You might like to try some of these yourself—you don't have to be a young girl to be interested in potential lovers—but be warned, some of them are pretty scary, designed to conjure up an apparition of the lover, rather than the warm-blooded version in person.

- At midnight on St. John's Eve, walk seven times sunwise around a church scattering hempseed and say, "*Hempseed I sow. Hempseed I sow. Let the one that is my true love come after me and mow.*" When you've completed the circuits, look over your left shoulder to see your true love coming after you . . . with a scythe!

- On Midsummer Eve take off your shift and wash it, turn it inside out, and hang it over the back of a chair in silence, near the fire. You will see your future husband, who will arrive to turn the shift at midnight.

- You can test whether a partner returns your love by following this ancient Roman method of divination: Take an apple and after eating it, take one seed and call it by your lover's name. Flick it from your finger with your thumbnail—if it hits the ceiling, your love is returned![1]

- Daisies are associated with faithful love and are sacred to the love goddesses Venus, Aphrodite, and Freya. Their folk name "measure of love" comes from the following charm: To find out whether someone loves you, take a daisy and pull off the petals one by one saying alternately, "He loves me, he loves me not," with each petal. The final petal will give you the answer.

- To discover when you will marry, find a meadow or lawn where daisies grow. Close your eyes and pull up a handful of grass. The number of daisies in the handful is the number of unmarried years remaining to you.

- One Welsh method of divination called *ffatio* involves washing clothes at midnight in a well, all the while chanting, *"Sawl ddaw I gyd-fydio, doed I gyd-ffatio"* (*"He who would my partner be, let him come and wash with me"*). The lover will then appear to help with the laundry.

- Walk around the church nine times and place a knife into the keyhole at the end of each round saying, *"Here is the knife. Where is the sheath?"* The symbolism of this is rather obvious and needs no comment!

- Fast on Midsummer Eve until midnight, then spread a supper of bread, cheese, and ale on a clean cloth and leave the front door wide open. Your future husband will enter the room, drink a glass of ale, bow, and leave. Or it might be a burglar.

Midsummer Eve Pillow Divinations

On Midsummer Eve, various herbs and charms placed beneath your pillow are capable of bringing prophetic dreams:

- To dream of an absent lover, daisy roots should be placed under the pillow.

- Place a piece of mugwort gathered on Midsummer Eve beneath your pillow for prophetic dreams.

- Wrap a piece of wax in a stocking and place it under the pillow. The next morning melt the wax and pour it into a vial of water to set in the sun. It will harden into a shape that shows the occupation of your future husband.

- Oak flowers on Midsummer Eve and withers before daybreak, it is said. Spread a sheet beneath the tree and catch the blossoms. Place them under your pillow and dream of your future lover.

- According to old English lore, yarrow gathered from a young man's grave and laid under the pillow on Midsummer Eve will produce a vision of your husband-to-be.[2]

- Placing ash leaves beneath the pillow results in prophetic dreams.

- A laurel leaf placed beneath the pillow brings about prophetic dreams.

- Betony placed beneath the pillow prevents nightmares, the elf sickness inflicted by malicious fairies, and even drunkenness.

- If you find a cinquefoil that has seven points (they usually have five), it should be placed under the pillow so that you can dream of your future partner.

- Place a four-leaf clover under your pillow to dream of your perfect partner.

- According to a northern English custom, a future spouse can be determined by putting three holly leaves, named for three suitors and blessed in the name of the Trinity,[3] under your pillow with the left hand. The first leaf to have turned over in the morning would be the one.

- Marigold petals placed under the pillow will give you prophetic dreams and enable you to identify a thief or robber.

- Mistletoe placed beneath the pillow is an aid to conception, and also ensures a restful sleep and good dreams.

- Placed under the pillow, rosemary ensures pleasant dreams and keeps evil away.

- Sleeping with sage leaves under the pillow encourages prophetic dreams.

Other Forms of Divination

Midsummer is one of the most potent nights for various forms of divination, a practice probably as old as humankind. Many methods of divination have been employed throughout the ages, including cards, tea leaves, palmistry, dominoes, dice, the I Ching, the reading of oracles, and the interpretation of dreams, oghams, and the runes. In modern times many new methods of divination have been invented, some based on old lore, and some not.

There are two types of diviners: One will go into a trance to make contact with the voices of the inner world, and the other will observe events, whether that be the flight of certain birds or the fall of the runes, which are then interpreted according to particular rules. The cosmos and its various concepts are presented as a series of symbols that are read according to their individual meanings and by their relationship to each other.

The Tarot

The tarot is a fortunetelling deck consisting of seventy-eight cards, divided into the major arcana and minor arcana. The twenty-two cards of the major arcana (described below) are known as the trump cards. The four suits of the minor arcana are the swords (the intellect), wands (energies), cups (the emotions), and disks (material matters). The cards are shuffled and laid out according to a variety of patterns, as desired by the reader.

Card	Key Word/ Energy	Image	Life Cycle	Spiritual Cycle
Fool	primal energy	young man on cliff/Green man	untutored beginnings	undirected energy
Magician/ High Priest	skill	man with magical tools	considered thought	awareness of being
High Priestess	mystery	priestess	awareness of psychic senses	awareness of mysteries beyond thought
The Empress/ The Lady	the Goddess	Mother Goddess with abundance of harvest	awareness of female side of personality	feminine energies
The Emperor/ The Lord	the God	man on throne	awareness of male side of personality	masculine energies
The Hierophant/ The Druid	polarity	pope	balancing of male and female aspects	polarity and balance
The Lovers	marriage (all)	two young lovers	love and choice	the sacred marriage of opposites/ polarities
Chariot	willpower	warrior in war chariot	self-discipline	self-discipline
Strength/ The Warrior	will	woman and lion/ warrior	personal strength and self-reliance	the development of the will

Card	Key Word/ Energy	Image	Life Cycle	Spiritual Cycle
Hermit/ Shaman	Otherworld	man with lantern	self-knowledge	Otherworld contact and teachers
Wheel	cosmic forces	the wheel of fortune	results of actions	awareness of cosmic forces
Justice/ The Web	karma	scales/web	responsibility of action	awareness of cosmic forces
Hanged Man	sacrifice	man hanging upside down	personal sacrifice	sacrifice of the ego
Death	death	skeletal figure/ Death Goddess	endings, change	death of the old self
Temperance/ Initiation/Art	initiation	figure pouring water/cauldron	the process of fundamental change is initiated, a catalyst	the death of the old self has cleared the way for the process of initiation to begin
Devil/ Underworld	subconscious	two figures chained to a rock with the devil in the background/Lord of the Underworld	repression, fears, inhibitions	facing the "demons" of the inner self
Tower	destruction	a tower struck by lightning	disasters	final dissolution of old self
Star	hope	a bright star	inspirations, broadening of horizons, hope	glimmerings of enlightenment
Moon	regeneration	a full moon	escape into dreams, failure to face reality	regeneration of new self
Sun	emergence	the midsummer sun	happiness, health, reward, achievement	consolidation of new self
Judgement	rebirth	figures emerging from a grave/ new risen sun	renewal, awakening, restoration of health and vitality	emergence of new self
World/ World Tree	totality	world/World Tree	culmination, completion of cycle, success	connection and interaction with the cosmos

The Medio Tarot Rite

Midsummer is the time to perform the Medio Tarot Rite. Three yellow or gold candles are placed on the table and lit. The major arcana cards are separated off from the pack and shuffled while saying:

Midsummer Night, Midsummer Night,
Season of witches, season of might
Show me the future, show me the past
Show me the first and show me the last
Grant me the vision, grant me the Sight
Grant me true knowledge this Midsummer Night!

The cards are laid out and read according to figure 1.

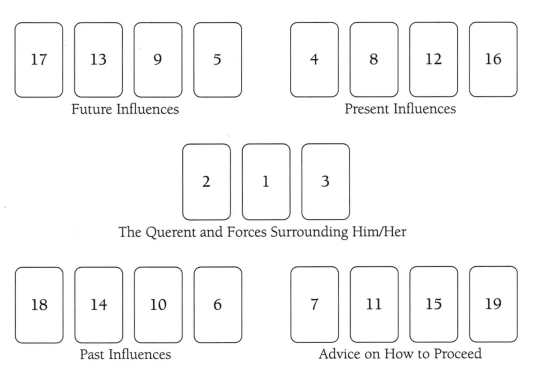

Figure 1: The Medio Tarot Layout

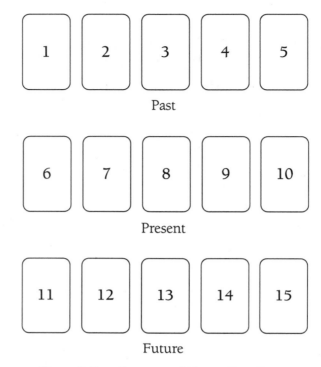

Past

Present

Future

Figure 2: Past, Present, and Future Tarot Layout

Past, Present, and Future Tarot Reading

A simple layout would be three rows of five cards to represent past, present, and future (see figure 2). This reading was made for Mandy on Midsummer Eve. She was uncertain about her future and felt that she had no control over it. The major arcana cards were separated from the deck. I asked her to think of her question while she was shuffling the cards.

Past

When the first row of cards was laid out, representing the past, we turned over the Hierophant, the High Priestess, the Wheel of Fortune reversed, the Emperor, and Strength reversed.

The Hierophant (also called the *Pope* or *Druid*) showed that new opportunities had arisen for Mandy, when she had the chance to put her own ideas and skills into practice.

The High Priestess (or *Female Pope*) revealed that her life was in the process of changing, perhaps in ways that were not yet completely clear. On the positive side, her intuitive powers were increasing, and she would be wise to listen to what her dreams and intuition were trying to tell her.

The Wheel of Fortune reversed indicated that she was resisting an inevitable change. What does not change stagnates, and it is impossible for things to always remain the same.

The Emperor (also called the *Lord*) indicated that Mandy had been trying to "fit in" rather than standing up for what she believed in and following her own path.

Strength (also called the *Warrior*) reversed indicated that Mandy was reacting with frustration and rage when she did not get her own way, being sulky and withdrawn. She felt powerless, angry, and not in control of her own life.

Present

Laying out the five cards representing the present, we found the Lovers reversed, the Magus reversed, the Hanged Man reversed, the Moon, and the Hermit.

The Lovers reversed indicated that Mandy was refusing to take responsibility for the consequences of her own actions, trying to lay the blame on others. The card indicated inner conflicts—she was at war with herself.

The Magus (also called *High Priest* or *Magician*) reversed indicated that Mandy was lacking in confidence, thinking that no one would be interested in what she had to say. She had a poor self-image and was reacting to situations with feelings of anger and helplessness.

The Hanged Man indicated that a willing sacrifice of some kind was called for. Mandy would be forced to recognize the necessity of change, which would involve letting go of one thing in order to gain another. This loss of control was very frightening to her, but fear was preventing her growth and the opportunity to discover new things and new experiences. She needed to relax and let events take their course.

The Moon card indicated a period of change and fluctuation, with nothing remaining stable or certain for long. This was frightening for Mandy, but the Moon called on her to accept change and the cycles of life. The card advised her to pay attention to her dreams and intuition—she should trust her instincts.

The Hermit (also called the *Shaman*) card indicated a time to show prudence, a time for careful planning, not action, a necessary period of isolation in which Mandy could come to know herself better and learn to rely on herself rather than others.

Future

The final spread of five cards, indicating the future, revealed Temperance reversed, Judgement reversed, the Tower, the Fool, and Justice. These cards showed Mandy's future if she continued on her present course.

Temperance (also called *Art* or *Initiation*) reversed indicated a lack of balance in Mandy's life. She was filling up her life with activities to disguise the fact that something fundamental was missing from it.

Judgement (also called *Rebirth*) reversed indicated that the time would come when Mandy would have to answer for her past decisions. She had not been true to herself and would have to suffer the consequences of her actions.

The Tower revealed that an unexpected shock or disaster would change Mandy's life completely. Actions, or lack of actions, taken in the past would have consequences that she had never imagined. Her tower would crack and fall because it was a flawed structure, built with the poor materials of fear, resentment, and false values. While the consequences of this card would be painful and unwanted, they would force Mandy to face up to the fact that she had been living her life on a false premise. Handled properly, this could be a card of liberation, depending on how she responded to the situation. She would have the opportunity to begin again, but if she tried to erect the same tower again from the old rubble, it would collapse.

The Fool (also called the *Green Man*) is raw, untamed energy, the primal chaos from which matter crystallizes and order emerges. This card showed that powerful forces were at work in Mandy's life, breaking down the old order so that a new one might emerge. She had already been discontented with her old life, but the change would be rapid and uncertain. Inevitably there would be a period of chaos, and she would have to leave her old life behind. However, a new and more vital life pattern would eventually emerge from the chaos.

The final card of Justice (or *Web*) related to Mandy's realization of herself as an individual, and the development of a personal morality and conscience, an inner sense of right and wrong. It advised that she would have to make a decision based on her own sense of what is right, rather than listen to the advice of others. Any action would have to be based on careful deliberation, considering its far-reaching effects on herself and others.

To sum up, in the past Mandy felt that she was not in control of her life. She was trying to go along with what others expected of her, not what she wanted herself. She was afraid to take advantage of opportunities when they presented themselves. This led to feelings of anger and frustration, though she blamed others for this, not herself.

The present cards revealed that Mandy was still refusing to take responsibility for her situation. She constantly felt angry and helpless. If she wanted to grow and progress, she had to let go of these feelings and stop trying to please others, and stand up for what she truly wanted and believed in. She should stand back and really listen to what her inner self was trying to tell her about her true path. Only in this way could she be happy.

The future cards revealed that if Mandy continued on her present course, and refused to take control of her own destiny, a time would come when the choice would be taken away from her. Something that seemed disastrous would occur, but this would be the catalyst that changed her life for the better. After a period of uncertainty and chaos, a new energy and direction would enter her life. She would realize herself as an individual, and recognize the value of her own thoughts and ideas.

Runes

The ancient peoples of northern Europe employed a system of divination called *runes*, marking slips of wood with angular symbols and throwing them onto a cloth before interpreting their fall. The word *rune* denotes something secret and may be translated as "to whisper," a meaning that still persists in modern Irish, where *rùn* means "secret" or "wish."[4] According to Norse lore, Odin, the chief god, was the first to gain knowledge of the runes. He seems to have been a shamanic figure and gained his knowledge by hanging from a tree, enduring pain and hunger for nine days and nights. Eventually he received a flash of insight in which he saw the runes and understood their use.

Each rune has its own meaning, describing something seemingly simple and ordinary: a torch, an ox, weather, trees, and so on. However, around this central object a wealth of concepts and symbols has accrued for which the rune is a kind of shorthand or direct link.

There are various types of runes, though the best known is the Elder Futhark, a Germanic set of twenty-four characters dating back to the fifth century C.E.[5] Latterly, these have been divided into three sets, or aettir, and assigned a god and goddess.

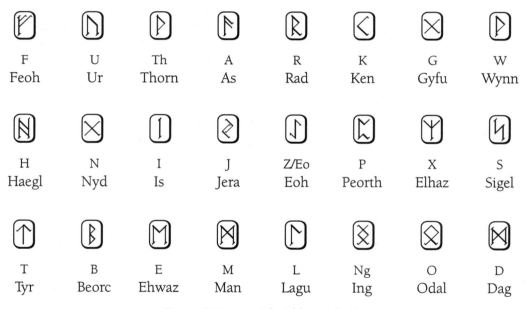

| F | U | Th | A | R | K | G | W |
| Feoh | Ur | Thorn | As | Rad | Ken | Gyfu | Wynn |

| H | N | I | J | Z/Eo | P | X | S |
| Haegl | Nyd | Is | Jera | Eoh | Peorth | Elhaz | Sigel |

| T | B | E | M | L | Ng | O | D |
| Tyr | Beorc | Ehwaz | Man | Lagu | Ing | Odal | Dag |

Figure 3: Runes—The Elder Futhark

Runes are readily available from occult stores and book shops, or you could make your own set from pebbles or glass beads painted with the runic symbols. My interpretation of the Elder Futhark is shown in figure 3.

First Aett
Ruled by Frey and Freya, god and goddess of fertility

Feoh	Cattle, wealth, money, a fee, beginnings, formation, creativity
Ur	Wild ox, untamed strength, perseverance, healing
Thorn	Thorn, magical protection, a protective barrier, Thor, creative energy
As	Mouth, god, divine power, divine breath, stability
Rad	A journey, wheel, motion, riding, moving forward
Ken	Torch fire, knowledge (kenning),[6] illumination
Gyfu	Gift, especially a gift of the gods (i.e., a talent), partnerships, balance
Wynn	Joy, success, prosperity, harmony

Second Aett
Ruled by Heimdall and Mordgud, guardian god and goddess

Haegl	Hail, formation, binding magic
Nyd	Need, necessity, binding magic, constraint
Is	Ice, immutability, binding magic, static time, delays
Jera	Harvest, completion in the proper season, the natural order is maintained
Eoh	Yew, bow, defense, sacrifice
Peorth	Dice cup, secret, divination, fate
Elhaz	Elk, power in defense, protection
Sigel	The sun, lightning flash, light, success, victory, happiness

Third Aett
Ruled by Tyr and Zisa, god and goddess of law and justice

Tyr	The god Tyr, justice, sword, power
Beorc	Birch, growth, fertility, purification
Ehwaz	Horse, change, transformation, movement, bonds, partnerships, travel
Man	A man or woman, a human being
Lagu	Water, fluidity, the flow of life, accepting the ebb and flow, increase and decrease
Ing	God of fertility, expansion
Odal	Inheritance, possessions, home, material wealth, connections with family
Dag	Day, light, illumination, balance of polarities, protection from harm

Reading the Runes

To perform a simple reading, place your runes into a bag and then one at a time draw out three or nine runes (3 x 3), representing the trends of past, present, and future.

Sample Runes Reading

Harry was frustrated that he seemed to be making no progress in his life. On Midsummer Eve he drew out three runes from the bag:

Haegl

The name of this rune means "hail," the frozen water that falls to earth from the heavens. It may damage crops and fruit, but is eventually transformed back into harmless water. This rune indicates delays or disruptions, but they are not always negative. This is also a rune of crystallization and formation, and Haegl the hailstone can be the mind seed that leads to dissatisfaction with life as it is, and the desire for change.

Jera

This rune represents the harvest or the turning of the year. The two complementary halves of this rune represent the dark half and the light half of the year—Hodur the dark god who is killed at the winter solstice and reborn at Midsummer, and Baldur the light god who is born at the winter solstice and killed at Midsummer. It indicates that the wheel is constantly turning, changing, moving on. The desire for change initiated in Haegl takes root. What is sown will be harvested, and previous actions will bear fruit.

As

This rune signifies a divine force at work. It is represented by the great ash tree Yggdrasil, which in Norse myth unites the realms of heaven, middle earth, and the underworld. It is the tree of Odin, who discovered the runes by hanging on it for nine days and nights, giving up one of his eyes in return for the knowledge.

Odin was the patron of poets and bards, and this rune represents intelligence, reason, and communication, perhaps from the gods themselves. Harry was being guided in his decisions and actions, if he would only listen to his intuition and take note of omens. This rune showed that he would be freed from his anxieties and those forces that held him back.

Playing Cards

There is a long tradition of using playing cards for divination, and these are especially useful if you do not have custom-made fortunetelling sets at hand. Only thirty-two cards are used (see below), so separate these from the deck. Cut and shuffle the cards. Lay out the first five cards in a row to represent the past, the second five cards in a row to represent the present, and the next five cards in a row to represent the future.

Hearts—emotional matters and relationships

Seven	Harmonious relationships and marriages
Eight	A journey
Nine	The matter will be resolved as you hope; this usually refers to a relationship
Ten	Unexpected success and great good fortune, especially in relationships
Jack	A male friend or lover who is charming but not to be trusted
Queen	A friendly, warm, fair-haired woman
King	A fair man who is generous and well-disposed toward you
Ace	Great happiness in the area of relationships; harmony and contentment; good news

Spades—intellectual matters and misfortunes

Seven	Quarrels and upsets
Eight	Bad news leading to unhappiness
Nine	Failure, bad luck
Ten	Bad news leading to anxiety or a journey
Jack	A dark, young man who is not to be trusted
Queen	A widow or divorcee who is scheming
King	A man of authority who is not what he seems
Ace	A business proposition or marriage proposal

Diamonds—money and practical matters

 Seven A surprising gift
 Eight A short, happy trip or excursion
 Nine News about money, business, or property
 Ten A marked change in the course of events
 Jack A messenger
 Queen A handsome woman who is nevertheless malicious
 King A capable, powerful man
 Ace Important news, probably in a letter

Clubs—creativity and spiritual matters

 Seven A small child influences you
 Eight A dark woman who brings joy
 Nine A good partnership or marriage
 Ten An unexpected legacy
 Jack A dark, young man who is sincere
 Queen A dark woman who is warm, affectionate, and well-meaning
 King A dark man who is helpful and kind
 Ace Success

Sample Playing Cards Reading

Lucy's brother had died abroad three months previously, leaving the family with a bureaucratic and legal tangle they were still trying to resolve.

Past

The first card drawn from the pack was the jack of diamonds, indicating a messenger. The eight of spades showed that he bore bad news, which lead to unhappiness. Lucy said that an official brought the news of her brother's death to the door. The ten of diamonds marked a change in the course of events as the family had make arrangements to travel abroad, as revealed by the ten of spades and the eight of hearts.

Present

The present cards revealed the disruptions that were still affecting the family. There were quarrels and upsets with the seven of spades, news of money and property relating to Lucy's brother's estate with the nine of diamonds, and a scheming female relative who was trying to gain control of the estate with the queen of diamonds. The king of clubs was identified as one of Lucy's uncles, who was trying to sort out all the problems and keep the family together.

Future

The ten of clubs indicated that Lucy would receive an unexpected legacy, confirmed by the seven of diamonds (a surprising gift). The ace of diamonds revealed that important news would arrive in a letter. She would meet a powerful man, represented by the king of diamonds, and receive an important business proposition (ace of hearts).

Ogham

This system of divination is based on old Celtic tree lore. The druids developed many methods of divination and augury, including this secret alphabet, known only to initiates. Each letter of the ogham alphabet represents a tree that has a wealth of mythology and symbolism associated with it. Some trees are mythologically important at certain times of the year, such as the oak at Midsummer or the hawthorn in May, when it flowers, but there is no evidence that the Celts ever used ogham as a tree calendar. The English poet Robert Graves invented this as a purely individual interpretation of the ogham alphabet.

You could make an ogham set by painting the ogham symbols (see figure 4) on pebbles or decorative glass stones, or by carving them on small tablets of wood. For a very simple set you could inscribe the symbols on squares of cardboard. For a very special set you could collect a stick from each ogham tree and carve the relevant ogham symbol onto it. As long as you prepare your oghams with thought and reverence and make them as beautiful as you can, the materials used do not matter—it's what you put into them that counts.

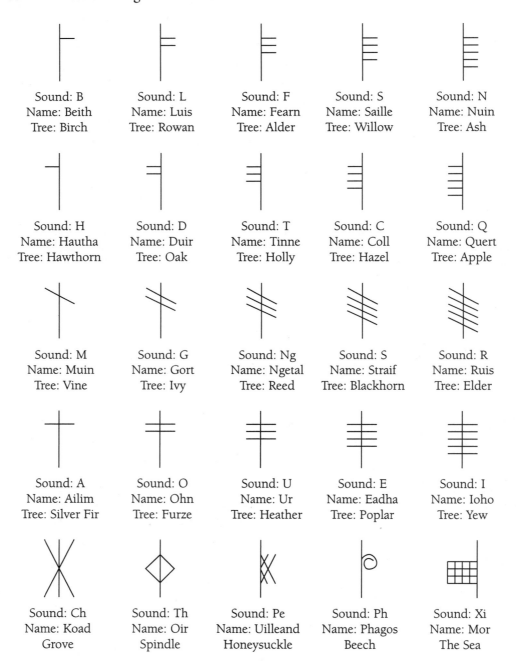

Figure 4: Oghams

Reading the Oghams

To read the oghams, place the tokens into a bag. One at a time, draw out nine tokens in three groups of three and place them in front of you. The first group represents the past, the second the present, and the third the future. When you have read the oghams, put them back into the bag and draw out three more tokens. These give guidance on mind, body, and spirit.

Beith—Birch: new beginnings, fertility, cleansing and purification, white magic

Luis—Rowan: protection, visions, oracles, inspiration, Imbolc

Fearn—Alder: renewal, regaining lost ground, healing

Saille—Willow: female magic, the Goddess, the rhythms of life, the moon

Nuin—Ash: axis mundi, linking of the realms, Otherworld travel

Huatha—Hawthorn: Beltane, fertility, flowering, sexual love

Duir—Oak: Midsummer, doorways to past and present, doorways to the mysteries, power, strength, nobility

Tinne—Holly: Yule, warrior magic, strength, battles, life, power

Coll—Hazel: wisdom, knowledge, autumn equinox

Quert—Apple: love, fulfillment, initiation, beauty, marriage

Muin—Vine: prophecy, truth, animal instincts

Gort—Ivy: visions, inner knowledge

Ngetal—Reed: action, strength, the sun, royalty, command, authority

Straif—Blackthorn: sorrow, strife, struggles, secrets

Ruis—Elder: Samhain, the Crone Goddess, occult knowledge and power

Ailim—Fir: motherhood, Mother Goddess, Yule, farsightedness

Ohn—Furze: Ostara, renewal, purification, sweet knowledge, poetic inspiration

Ur—Heather: healing, self-discovery, messages from the Otherworld

Eadha—White poplar: protection from illness, rebirth

Ioho—Yew: endings and beginnings, renewal from the darkest depths

Koad—Grove: sacred place, magic circle, home

Oir—Spindle: secrets uncovered, knowledge gained in unexpected sources

Uilleand—Honeysuckle: that which is hidden, knowledge to be worked for

Phagos—Beech: knowledge from books, old knowledge proves useful

Mor—The sea: travel, the unconscious mind

Sample Ogham Reading

This reading was undertaken for Tabitha, a witch who had been suffering from a serious illness for several years, but was slowly recovering. During this time all her inner resources had been called upon to see her through the crisis.

Past

Fearn   This ogham indicated that within the past couple of years Tabitha's healing had really begun. It revealed that a powerful cycle of renewal and restoration was in progress.

Phagos   This is the rune of old knowledge put into practice, and Tabitha had called upon many of her own Craft skills and the abilities of her fellow witches to bring about her healing.

Tinne   This ogham revealed Tabitha's struggles and battles with her illness, and the depression it sometimes engendered, but also the strength, life, and power she was able to draw upon.

Present

Uilleand   This rune indicates secrets and hidden knowledge that must be worked for.

Oir   This rune indicates secrets uncovered, knowledge gained in unexpected places, sudden insight, and also delight and joy.

Ioho   This rune, represented by the yew tree, reveals renewal from the depths of darkness, and new beginnings.

As we talked about the meaning of these runes, Tabitha revealed that she felt that out of the darkness and despair of her illness and suffering, she had gained new and much deeper insights into the mysteries of life, her path, and her Craft. This knowledge was still unfolding, and she felt there was much more to come.

Future

Mor   This is the ogham of the sea, travel, and journeys, or sometimes the unconscious mind symbolized by the great ocean. Tabitha felt this was denoting a spiritual journey, rather than a physical one.

Eadha   This ogham was particularly welcome for Tabitha, meaning protection from illness and a physical rebirth, suggesting that she will regain her health and not slip back into sickness once again.

Duir   This is the ogham of the oak tree and represents a mysterious doorway, the entrance to the mysteries. It showed that the revelations begun in the dark time of Tabitha's illness were still unfolding. It is an ogham of great power and strength.

These three oghams indicated that Tabitha's healing will continue, as will her journey into knowledge. Next we drew three runes to denote mind, body, and spirit.

The Mind ogham drawn was Coll, or hazel, a very fortunate ogham for this position, indicating wisdom and knowledge.

The Body ogham was revealed as Nuin, the ash tree. In Celtic and Norse lore the ash tree links the three worlds of heaven, earth, and the underworld. This ogham indicated that Tabitha was gaining profound knowledge of the link between the inner and outer realms, and this knowledge was part of her healing process.

A lovely ogham was drawn in the Spirit position—Quert, or the apple tree. This indicated spiritual joy and fulfillment, love, beauty, and a new level of initiation.

Fairy Contact

Midsummer Eve is one of the three great fairy festivals, the other two being Halloween and May Eve.[7] All sorts of enchantments are in the air. Spirits and fairies are abroad until St. Peter's Day (June 29), moving among humankind, frolicking around the Midsummer bonfires, and playing all sorts of tricks ranging from innocent pranks to inflicting horrible curses and even death on those who offend them. It is at this time that they most often steal away human women to become their brides.[8] They love to visit certain magical places, such as the Rollright Stones in Oxfordshire, England, where they pop out of a hole near the King Stone and dance around the circle.

The following are fairy folk who are particularly active at Midsummer:

Robin Goodfellow—The mischievous fairy named Robin Goodfellow, Jack Robinson, or Puck plays tricks on the unwary who dare to venture out into wild and lonely places on such an enchanted night. He is believed to light the Midsummer bonfires himself. He is sometimes described as the jester of the fairy court and appears in this role in Shakespeare's *A Midsummer Night's Dream*. In parts of Worcestershire peasants claimed to be "Poake led" into ditches and bogs by the mysterious fairy before it disappeared with a loud laugh. In the Midlands this was called being "pouk-ledden" and is similar to being pixy-led.

Robin Goodfellow is sometimes described as having the head of a youth and the body of a goat. Like the god Pan, he has a lusty nature, small horns on his head, and carries musical pipes. It may be that he is the fairy remnant of the ancient horned god or nature spirits, since there originally seem to have been a race of pucks. He is never seen between Halloween and the vernal equinox and is usually accompanied by a variety of animals.

Robin Goodfellow is related to the Welsh Pwca and the Irish Phooka, the Norwegian Pukje, the Danish Puge, the Swedish Puke, the old Norse Puki, the Latvian Pukis, the German Puks, and the Baltic Puk.

Selkies—In the Shetlands those strange and lovely creatures called *selkies* come ashore on Johnsmas Eve. They normally have the appearance of gray seals, but shed their skins to become human on this night. Once ashore and in human form, the selkie-folk will dance on the seashore, and if they are disturbed they will grab their skins and run back to the sea. If a man can steal and hide the shed skin, he can force a selkie maid to marry him, though if she ever finds her skin she will put it on and be off back to the sea. Descendants of such unions have webbed fingers and toes or a horny substance on their palms and soles. The Mac Codrum clan from North Uist claim descent from selkies; they are known as *Sliochd nan Ron*, the "Offspring of Seals." A distant ancestor stole the skin of a seal maiden as she danced and kept it hidden for many years, during which time she bore him many children.

Tales of seal people are found all over Shetland, Orkney, and the Hebrides and Faeroe islands. Seals are a common sight in these parts, and the name of Orkney is derived from the Norse *Orkneyjar,* meaning "Seal Islands."

Oakmen—At this time of year, when the oak is the most powerful tree totem, spirits called *oakmen* guard it. These are the most widespread tree fairies in England. Beware, because they are fierce guardians of their trees and do not really like humans. They appear as forest dwarfs and offer food to passing mortals, but this always turns out to be poisonous fungi disguised by glamour, the fairy magic. They also guard all the forest animals, especially foxes, and punish those who harm them. The rain that gathers in their oak hollows has powerful healing qualities.

Pilwiz—In Germany the pilwiz fairies are busy trying to steal the growing grain. They raid cornfields, fixing sickles to their huge toes to cut the corn. To stop this, a farmer must catch the pilwiz in the act on St. John's Day, but if the pilwiz should see the farmer first, the man will die.

Rusalka—These Slavic and Russian nymphs walk the land at Midsummer, and where they walk flowers appear. They are associated with fertility, and when they move through the grain it causes it to grow. They have long, green hair and swing on the branches of forest trees. Rusalka have power over the wind and rain and may once have been weather deities.

Spunkies—In Somerset, England, these little fairies appear like will-o'-the-wisps, carrying candles and leading travelers astray at night. On Midsummer Eve they go to the churchyard to meet the newly dead. Some say that the spunkies themselves are the souls of unbaptized children, condemned to wander until doomsday.

Trows—These Shetland fairies come in two varieties: land trows and sea trows. Both are small, squat fairies with an aversion to daylight. Trows can be seen performing a lopsided crouching and hopping dance called *Henking,* especially at Midsummer, which is one of their great festivals. Sometimes they invite humans into their mounds, and sometimes they steal away women of loose morals to act as wet-nurses to trow children, which are called *trowlings.*

Aine—The fairy Aine was sitting one day by Lough Gur, Ireland, when the Earl of Desmond chanced to see her and instantly fell in love with her. She agreed to marry him on the condition that he would never be surprised by anything that their children did. Unfortunately, when their son, the Earl of Fitzgerald, jumped in and out of a bottle, he couldn't help his amazement, and poor Fitzgerald turned into a wild goose and flew away, while Aine fled into the mound still known as Cnoc Aine. Her feast day is Midsummer Eve, when she appears at the mound, surrounded by maidens.

The Elder Mother—The elder tree is sacred to elves and fairies. A spirit inhabits the tree, and for this reason when it is cut at Midsummer it bleeds real blood. In Denmark the elder is under the protection of the fairy/goddess Hulda, and in England the Elder Mother or Elder Queen. She lives at its roots and is the mother of the elves. According to Danish lore, if you stand under an elder on Midsummer Eve you will see the King of the Elves pass by.[9] In Lincolnshire, England, it was thought that cutting elder wood without leave of the Old Lady or Old Girl offended her, so permission must be sought:

> *Owd Gal, give me some of thy wood and Oi will give thee some of moine,*
> *when I graws inter a tree.*

Amadan-na-Briona—The Irish spirit the Amadan-na-Briona is at his most active at Midsummer, playing mischievous tricks on people. Also called "The Fool of the Forth," he changes his shape every two days. When he appears as a man he is very wide and wears a high hat, though he has been known to appear as a sheep with a beard. If you meet him you should say, "The Lord be between us and harm," because if he touches you he will inflict an incurable madness or even death.[10] He knocks on doors late at night, throwing basins after people or popping up from behind hedges.

To See Fairies

Traditionally the best time to see fairies is on Midsummer Eve. Wreaths of eerie mist often surround fairy mounds, fairy rings, stone circles, and other magical places. Should you find a gap in the mist, you will be able to pass through into the Otherworld. On this night the fairy mounds open and they may be seen feasting inside. To find the entrance to a fairy hill, you should walk nine times around it. Sometimes a procession of lights can be seen moving from one hill to another, and this is the fairies moving house or visiting their neighbors. They use well-trodden paths running in straight lines between the mounds. Any building on one of these fairy ways will meet with disturbances.

It was on Midsummer Eve that St. Levan saw the fairy gardens near Logan Rock in Cornwall:

When I have been to sea close under the cliffs, of a fine summer's night, I have heard the sweetest music, and seen hundreds of little lights moving about among what looked like flowers. Ay! And they are flowers too, for you may smell the sweet scent far out at sea. Indeed, I have heard many of the old men say that they have smelt the sweet perfume and heard the fairy music from the fairy gardens of the castle when more than a mile from the shore.

Those who have seen the gardens in the midsummer moonlight say they are covered with flowers of every color, all more brilliant than any mortal flower.

Fairy kingdoms exist in a different dimension than that of humankind, though they sometimes appear for a brief instant to mortal eyes. There is a square of turf in Wales where, if you trip over it, you will get a single glimpse of fairies, though the spot can never be found twice.

Fairies can become visible or invisible at will, or be visible to one person while being invisible to another, though sometimes they can be spied at their revels unawares. You must gaze steadily to see fairies—if you blink they will disappear. They are most often seen at noon, midnight, or twilight.

If you want to see fairies, then you will need the aid of certain magical herbs such as thyme and primrose. The Sight can be opened by a four-leaf clover, as the milkmaid who accidentally picked a four-leaf clover with the grass she used to soften the weight of the pail on her head discovered. When next she looked at her cow, she saw dozens of fairies milking it. An old recipe to make a potion to enable you to see fairies ran thus:

Take a pint of Sallet oil and put it in a glasse, first washing it with rose water.
Then put thereto the budds of hollyhocke, of marygolde,
of young hazle and the topps of wild thyme.
Take the grasse of a fairy throne; then all these put into the glasse . . .
dissolve three dayes in the sunne, and keep it for thy use.[11]

You may note that the recipe includes wild thyme. If you can find a bed of wild thyme, the King of the Fairies will visit this to dance there with his followers at midnight on Midsummer Eve. Wild thyme is an ingredient of many magical potions, dating from around 1600, that allow those who take them to see fairies. One simple charm is to make a brew of wild thyme tops gathered near the side of a fairy hill plus grass from a fairy throne.[12] Anoint your eyes with it. Wild thyme is unlucky if brought indoors.

A simpler spell involves gathering fern seeds at midnight on Midsummer Eve and rubbing them on your eyelids. The fairy folk are also particularly fond of rosemary, and the incense attracts them. Pour a libation of rosemary infusion (see chapter 5) on a fairy-haunted spot to please them.

The Good Folk often inhabit woody dells, concealing themselves among the flowers of the foxglove.[13] Growing foxgloves in your garden will attract fairies, or if you want to keep fairies away, you should weed them out. Like other fairy flowers, it is unlucky to take them indoors.

In Brittany the rite of Sounding the Basins (*senin ar c'hirinou*) is undertaken at Midsummer to conjure up the wildfolk. Pebbles and coins were placed into a copper basin and this was shaken.

Protection from Mischievous Fairies

While you might like to meet some happy and friendly fairies, there are other fairies who like to play cruel and malicious tricks on humans at Midsummer. Their favorite prank is to lead travelers away from their path; this is called *being pixy-led*.

Other fairies try to frighten people, steal away young girls for brides, shoot harmful elf bolts at those who intrude on fairy territory, or even lay dreadful curses that bring illness and death. It may be necessary to take precautions against the attentions of such spiteful creatures.

- According to Irish lore, fairies try to pass around the baal fires in a whirlwind in order to extinguish them, but they may be kept off by throwing fire at them.
- Humans can protect themselves from fairies by leaping through the baal fire.
- Cattle are protected from the attentions of evil spirits by driving them through the embers of the baal fire.[14]
- Cross a stream of running water to elude fairy pursuers.
- Carry a bit of rue in your pocket to keep evil spirits at bay.
- If fairies are troubling you or if you are being pixy-led, turn your clothes inside out and this will confuse them long enough to allow you to make your escape.
- If a friend has been dragged into a fairy ring, toss one of your gloves inside and the revelers will disperse.
- To keep fairies out of your bedroom, scatter flax on the floor.
- Fairies are terrified of iron and they will vanish immediately on being shown any form of the metal. Keep a knife or a nail in your pocket and under your pillow at night.
- A Hag Stone (a naturally holed stone) hung up by the door or in the barn will keep bad fairies away.
- Rowan wood crosstied with red thread will offer protection when hung in a high place in the house or barn.
- The besom placed beside the hearth will prevent fairies from coming down the chimney.
- A Witch Bottle (a glass bottle containing sharp objects such as nails and pins, ashes, salt, and rowan wood) can be buried before the doorstep.

- If oatmeal is sprinkled on clothes or carried in the pocket, no bad fairy will approach.

- St. John's wort prevents the fairies from carrying off people while they sleep.

- A mulberry tree in your garden will keep away evil fairies. At the dangerous time of Midsummer, you should dance around it counterclockwise. This is possibly the origin of the rhyme "Here We Go Round the Mulberry Bush."

Charging Crystals

Midsummer is the best time to charge your crystals magically with the powerful energies of the sun. The Celts associated clear quartz with the sun, calling it *grian-choichit,* or "sunstone." To them, a crystal was solidified light. This is why fairy women and goddesses are often said to live in crystal palaces or glass castles. The Celts dipped quartz crystals into the water of healing wells to bring extra healing energies into the stones. Crystals were also dropped into such wells as offerings to the resident goddesses to solicit cures.

The stones of standing stones and stone circles always have large deposits of quartz within them. These, too, are charged with the rising of the sun at the solstice.

Cleansing and Charging a Crystal

Crystals absorb the energies and emotions surrounding them, so before you use a stone it must be cleansed of these. Hold your crystals under running water. As you do so, visualize any negativity being washed away. Place the crystals on a nonmetal tray and put them outside in your garden or on your windowsill to catch the rays of the rising sun. Do not lay them directly on the ground, as any charge will be earthed straight away. Allow them to remain in place all day, absorbing the solar energies, and then bring them in at dusk.

Programming a Crystal

A crystal can only be programmed for one purpose at a time. Find a place where you can sit undisturbed, and spend some time examining the crystal. When you feel you know your crystal well, close your eyes and relax. Visualize a white light coming from the earth beneath your feet, rising up your back and over your head, traveling down your front, and enclosing you in sphere of protective light. Hold the crystal against your forehead and call to mind the purpose with which you wish to charge it, perhaps healing for a friend, or to help you meditate. Once charged and programmed, the stone should be set in a secure place where it will not be disturbed. If you want to use it for something else at a later time, you will have to cleanse, charge, and program it all over again. Each gem has its own properties.

Gem Properties

Agate—A variety of chalcedony (composed of chert and fine quartz) with colored bands or other markings, found in Britain, the United States, and India. It was first found on the banks of the river Achates, hence the name. An agate amulet increases self-confidence and makes the bearer eloquent. It improves vitality. It attracts good friends and has been used by many powerful people over the centuries for this purpose, notably Queen Elizabeth I. The agate is also a truth talisman. Place it on the left breast of a sleeping woman and she will tell you whatever you wish to know.[15]

Amazonite—Composed of potassium feldspar, a light-green variety of microline with white flecks. It is found in New England, Colorado, and Brazil, among other places. It was prized by the ancient Egyptians to calm the mental state and emotional disorders. It is good for healing and spiritual growth, as well as for enhancing the properties of other gems and essential oils.

Amber—Not a stone, but a translucent, fossil tree resin formed millions of years ago. It is pale yellow or brownish in color, often with bits of plants or insects trapped within. It is found in Britain, Sicily, Siberia, Greenland, and the United States, but most amber comes from the Baltic region, where the amber-producing pines were submerged beneath the sea. Storms may cause pieces of amber to be washed up on beaches, but most amber is mined. The Norse believed that amber was the tears of the love goddess Freya, shed into the sea when her husband Odur (the summer sun) left her in the winter. Amber acquires a negative electrical charge when it is rubbed, and was called *elekton* by the ancient Greeks—from this we get our word *electricity*. Amber will carry a magical charge, and as such forms part of the witches' traditional necklace (along with jet). Necklaces or amulets of amber are worn around the neck to protect the wearer from many diseases, especially fever, rheumatism, throat and neck infections, thyroid problems and disease,[16] and weakness of the eyes. Looking through amber strengthens the sight. A piece of red amber is excellent for protection against the evil eye and enchantment.

Amethyst—A purple quartz found mostly in Brazil. In ancient times it was worn as an amulet to prevent drunkenness or was taken in potions to cure poisoning and sterility. When worn it is said to make you witty and improve your memory, bring you good luck, and ensure the constancy of a lover. If a man wears it, good women will love him. Placed under your pillow or near your bed, it will help you fall asleep and bring you good dreams. It brings harmony and balance and eases emotional despair and grief. It emits a purifying energy that calms the nervous system. It aids meditation. Rub an amethyst on the forehead to help relieve a headache. Wear an amethyst to help asthma and lung problems. An amethyst will help protect you from psychic attack.

Apache Tear Drop—A form of obsidian, a type of volcanic glass. These stones are lucky, and it is said that those who possess one will never have to shed tears again.

Aquamarine—A pale blue-green stone, a type of beryl that helps foster visions and clairvoyant faculties. A good-luck charm for interviews and exams. Helpful for the eyes, liver, throat, and stomach. Aquamarine promotes logical thinking.

Aventurine—A quartz stone composed of silica with some impurities. It has a dark-green, metallic appearance and is found in India, China, and Brazil. It brings luck in love and games. The stone is good for skin diseases and the complexion, and it affects the pituitary gland, the muscles, and the nervous system. Aventurine also relieves migraines and soothes the eyes. Leave a piece in water overnight and wash your eyes with the

water the next morning. The water can also be used for skin irritations. Aventurine aids visualization and is a good stone for artists, writers, and creative people in general. The green of the gem attracts wealth, so aventurines can be used in money spells.

Beryl—An opaque or transparent green or yellow stone. In the medieval period, beryls were made into amulets to hinder lust in the unmarried, bring about love and harmony between married couples, and to help the bearer win arguments, gain awareness, become courteous, and deter enemies. The ancient Egyptians used it to heal the thyroid gland and to energize the lazy. Help relieve swollen glands by rubbing them with a beryl. If you gaze into a beryl, you may be able to see the future, as it stimulates visionary capacities. The ancients called it "the seer's stone."

Bloodstone—A greenish jasper with red marks formed from iron oxide, resembling blood, found in India, Australia, Brazil, China, and the United States. The ancient Tibetans used it to staunch blood. It helps detoxify the physical body. Worn as an amulet, it brings fame and a long life. Sleep with a bloodstone under your pillow to have dreams of the future. It is also called *heliotrope*, and it was once believed that if you covered the stone with the herb heliotrope, you would become invisible.

Blue Lace Agate—Banded chalcedony, pale blue with paler markings, found in southwest Africa. It strengthens the power of the sun in your zodiac sign when worn. It also helps you speak, sharpens the sight, and illuminates the mind. It fosters inner peace.

Cairngorm—Also called *smoky quartz* or *scots topaz*, this powerful type of quartz is colored gray by the natural radioactivity in the crystal bed. It is used to achieve visions.

Carbuncle—A red gem, usually a garnet, of round shape (garnets are usually faceted) that was once believed to prevent poisoning when worn as an amulet. The carbuncle also hinders lust, sadness, and bad dreams. It keeps the bearer healthy, but if he or she does become ill, the stone will fade. The darker-colored stones are considered masculine, while the paler ones are considered feminine. The ancient Egyptians and tribesmen of northern India used them to staunch wounds. Carbuncles can help banish sadness and bring peace of mind to those unjustly accused, and assist with reconciliation.

Carnelian—Also called *cornelian*, carnelian is a variety of chalcedony found in India and South America. It comes in a number of shades, from pale orange to red, though the red was most highly prized by the ancients. It symbolizes good luck and contentment. This stone can be worn against skin diseases. It calms anger, and helps develop fluent speech and courage. It is good for the absent-minded, the confused, or the unfocused. It strengthens the voice. Carnelian helps cleanse the liver—hold one over the area. Hold one over the stomach to ease menstrual cramps. It draws energy into the physical body, and is therefore useful for those suffering from fatigue. Magically it represents the elements of both fire and earth. It is helpful to those under psychic attack when worn in the umbilical region, as recommended by the ancient Egyptian Book of the Dead.

Chalcedony—A pale, translucent quartz, sometimes milky white. Wear one to be lucky in love, happy, carefree, and strong. This gem is useful in the relief of depression, and will help you overcome self-delusion and sharpen your self-knowledge. In Italy white chalcedony is made into necklaces and worn to increase a nursing mother's milk.

Chrysolite—A transparent variety of magnesium iron silicate, yellow or greenish in color. The bright-green sort is called *peridot*, while the olive shade is called *olivine*. It was much favored by the Arabs, who considered it to be of more value than diamonds. It stills fear, especially fear of heart irregularities. An old spell states that if you bore a hole in the stone and fill it with hairs from the mane of an ass and wear it on the left arm, you will be free from melancholy, foolishness, and fear. It also helps ease asthma and lung disease.

Chrysoprase—A variety of quartz, usually apple green in color. The stone is worn as an amulet for happiness and to strengthen the eyes. The ancients thought that it helped eliminate covetous thoughts and envy, while stimulating the desire for success. Alexander the Great wore one. The stone activates clairvoyant faculties.

Citrine—A pale-yellow quartz, the citrine helps control emotions.

Coral—Made from the skeletal matter of particular marine animals, coral is not really a gemstone. Worn as an amulet, it prevents enchantment and the evil eye. It preserves the bearer from his or her own foolishness. Red coral loses its color when its owner is ill. Coral is used to strengthen the heart and spleen. The collection of coral is very damaging to the environment, so you should only buy antique coral jewelry.

Crazy Lace Agate—A white, paisley-patterned cryptocrystalline stone found in Mexico. The ancients wore it to placate the gods and inspire courage. It sharpens the sight, helps the eyes, illuminates the mind, gives vitality, and makes you eloquent. It strengthens the ego, improves self-esteem, gives a feeling of consolation, and helps banish fear.

Diamond—A brilliant gem that may be used in an amulet to procure fame and fortune and prevent witchcraft. Because of its hardness it also endows the bearer with strength and invulnerability and brings victory when worn on the left arm. The diamond is a talisman for reconciling husbands and wives who have quarreled. Fastened to the left arm touching the skin, it keeps away nocturnal fears. It inspires courage and intensifies the properties of the gems it is set with, particularly amethyst and emerald. The ancients used diamonds to purify rooms and create a sterile atmosphere.

Emerald—A form of green beryl. An emerald amulet brings the wearer wealth, good fortune, and the ability to foretell the future. It banishes evil spirits. Worn in a ring, emerald helps poor memory and dizziness. Emeralds intensify the innate characteristics of a person for good or ill.

Flint—A flint worn as an amulet keeps away evil spirits and nightmares. According to an old spell, you can cast flint stones behind your back toward the west to bring rain.

Garnet—A type of carbuncle revered by the ancients for its ability to warn of danger—it goes dull when danger threatens. Garnets treat blood disorders and skin diseases. Garnets help you work through long-term resentments.

Haematite—A form of black crystalline iron, found in Britain, Norway, Sweden, and around Lake Superior. It is used to protect the wearer from enchantment, negative energies, and psychic attack.

Hag Stone—To cure disease, affliction by nightmare, or bewitchment, hang a hag stone with a natural hole in it over the bed of the sufferer. Small hag stones that have natural holes in them are excellent amulets against disease and the evil eye.

Jacinth—A red-orange or yellow zircon. An amulet worn around the neck will protect you from enchantment, make you lucky in money and business matters, and keep you cheerful and alert. Deep-yellow jacinth will help relieve depression. Give one as a gift to win someone's affection. The sun rules this stone.

Jade—Also called *nephrite*, jade is a green, lavender, or whitish mineral. It is especially prized in China as the most magical stone and called "the jewel of the gods." Jade is made into amulets for long life, good health, and to prevent misfortune. For a long life, eat from a jade bowl. Jade is protective and prevents nightmares. It is helpful for kidney complaints.

Jasper—Opaque quartz, usually green, worn as an amulet against dysentery, nightmares, and hallucinations.

Jet—A deep-black stone of lignite (coal), agate, or marble. It is found in Whitby (Yorkshire, England) and Spain. It is sacred to the goddess Cybele and the planet Saturn. It strengthens spiritual vigor, and monks and nuns wore bracelets of it. It is a traditional mourning stone; Queen Victoria wore a great deal of jet after the death of Prince Albert. Jet drives away hallucinations. In Ireland, it is said to have eight virtues: it protects from thunder, demons, poison, possession by evil spirits, snake bite, sorcery, and disease, and gives a smooth body.

Lapis Lazuli—A deep-blue gem worn as an amulet to cure melancholy.

Lodestone—Also called *loadstone*, lodestone is a variety of magnetite, composed of oxides of iron. It is a magnetic stone that attracts iron. The lodestone can enable you to foretell the future and will endow you with divine inspiration and secret knowledge. To cure yourself of disease, shake a lodestone in your hands. Worn as an amulet, the lodestone reconciles lovers' quarrels. It helps liver problems and gout.

Malachite—Contains a great deal of copper, which makes it green. The ancients recommended it for colic, cramps, and rheumatism. It helps tone muscles and prevents cramps in the intestines.

Moonstone—This variety of feldspar is a translucent, pale stone in a variety of shades. It is found in Ceylon and Brazil. The gem has affinities with the energies of the moon. It is receptive and helps balance and soothe the emotions. It aids in the attainment of peace and calm, hormonal equilibrium in women, and helps men tune into their feminine side. It is a powerful stone for magicians and witches as it will hold a magical charge, act as a link to a spirit guide, and aid in the development of clairvoyance and other psychic powers.

Opal—A species of soft quartz, noncrystalline silica found in muddy areas and on the surface in Australia. The iridescent colors are caused by water trapped in the minute fissures within the stone. They are sacred to Venus, the Roman goddess of love. It is said that if an opal wearer deceives another in love, or abuses a lover, the stone will bring the wearer bad luck. The ancients called the opal the "tears of the moon." Opals are believed to change color according to the emotions of the wearer, becoming dull if the wearer is ill or depressed. They were used in ancient times for the treatment of eye diseases, and the Roman name for the gem meant "eye-stone."

Pearl—Pearls are formed inside oysters as a reaction to an irritant. Wear a pearl as an amulet for longevity, though pearls have a reputation for bringing bad luck or tears.

Pebble—To rid yourself of warts, bury as many pebbles as you have warts. Black, kidney-shaped pebbles bring health and fortune, and protection against the evil eye. Stones shaped naturally like a couple embracing are charms that bring love. Heat a stone until it is red hot and throw it into a basin of water (be sure to stand back when you do this!). This water will then be good for bathing bruises.

Quartz—Quartz is one of the most
abundant minerals on the planet,
formed from oxygen and silicon.
The purest form is rock crystal, or
clear quartz. When quartz contains impurities, such as sodium
or lithium, then other gemstones are
formed, such as amethyst, rose quartz,
and cat's-eye. The points are considered masculine and energizing, while milky quartz is feminine and calming.

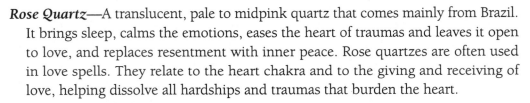

Rose Quartz—A translucent, pale to midpink quartz that comes mainly from Brazil.
It brings sleep, calms the emotions, eases the heart of traumas and leaves it open
to love, and replaces resentment with inner peace. Rose quartzes are often used
in love spells. They relate to the heart chakra and to the giving and receiving of
love, helping dissolve all hardships and traumas that burden the heart.

Ruby—A crimson-colored precious stone, a ruby is a form of transparent red
corundum found in clay soil in Myanmar, Thailand, Sri Lanka, Afghanistan, and
North Carolina. The ruby becomes dark or cloudy when evil threatens. Wear it to
remain pure in thought. It induces calm, dispels fears, drives away evil, excites
sexuality, invigorates the root chakra, and strengthens a good relationship and
splits apart a bad one.

Sapphire—A blue variety of corundum that is worn as an amulet to prevent fever,
excessive perspiration, eye disease, injury, and poison. This is *the* stone for those
who seek spiritual enlightenment, it helps develop powers of concentration. Sap-
phires are initiate's stones, awarded for achievement. A sapphire should not be pur-
chased for yourself, but should always be a gift. They bring tranquillity, good
health, courage, and peace of mind, and protect from envy, treachery, and captivity.

Sardonyx—A reddish-brown base surmounted by a layer of white chalcedony. Sardonyx was often used to make cameos, and it protects the wearer from infectious
diseases, aids the memory, and makes a cranky person more agreeable.

Snowflake Obsidian—A form of volcanic siliceous rock, black with white markings that look like snowflakes. It sharpens internal and external vision, reveals the ego, and symbolizes polarity.

Sodalite—A rich, dark-blue stone composed of chloric aluminum silicate. It is mostly found in Canada and Brazil. This gemstone helps prolong physical endurance and creates inner harmony. It is good for the oversensitive and helps clear away destructive, old mental patterns. Meditate with the stone placed over the third eye to awaken it.

Spinal—This stone is also known as the *star ruby* and comes in many colors—red, orange, green, and violet. It has a gentle energy and was favored in Chaldea and India. It is used to prevent nightmares, chills, and flu. It energizes the spleen.

Star Ruby—See *spinal.*

Star Sapphire—Also called *asteria sapphire*. The white sapphire possesses six rays of light in the upper part of the stone. It brings peace to the troubled mind and is also called the *Star of Peace*. Pope Innocent III decreed the pope's ring should be a white star sapphire set in gold.

Tiger's-Eye—A form of crystallized quartz sometimes called "imprisoned sunlight," this gem has a yellow stripe running through it. It stimulates courage, eases nightmares, and helps you keep what you possess. It is worn to avert the evil eye and to help cure eye diseases, and it aids inner sight and helps you see your own faults. It fosters the development of courage and inner strength, engenders a sense of responsibility, and helps you overcome negativity.

Topaz—A gem of aluminum silicate, topaz comes in many colors. It is worn as an amulet for wisdom, wealth, and beauty, and against lust and greed. The orange variety stimulates courage, joy, and contentment. The ancient Egyptians used it to treat asthma. Placed on the forehead, it eases a troubled mind, nerves, and insomnia. Topaz has a great affinity with the sun.

Tourmaline—These stones vary in color from black through green, pink, yellow, blue, white, and red. A rare type contains three separate colors in its makeup. A tourmaline possesses both positive and negative poles electrically. It will restore physical vitality after nervous exhaustion, and help overcome melancholy, fear, and negative thoughts. Wearing one attracts favors and friendship.

Turquoise—A blue-green stone worn as an amulet for good fortune and against the evil eye. Turquoise changes color according to the health of its owner, while protecting him or her from accidents. It brings together a man and wife who have quarreled. The ancients called it the *Celestial Stone*, as it could protect the wearer from enmity. Wear turquoise when suffering from grief to bring peace. When set in silver, the qualities of turquoise are enhanced. It is known as the *stone of Venus*.

Unikite—A pink-and-green feldspar and epidote, opaque stone found in North Carolina and Tennessee. It awakens love in the heart chakra, and heals emotional hurt. It helps balance the emotions.

The Wand

The most propitious time in the year to make a magic wand is at Midsummer. The wand is the tool that joins the physical and spiritual realms and transmits energy from one to the other. The wand relates to the element of fire, creativity, life energy, and the spirit. It focuses and directs the magical will to make it manifest in the world. It is the magical tool connected with the season of summer, noonday, and the direction of the south. In the Celtic tradition the wand comes from the magical city of the south, Finias.

Making a Wand

You should cut your own wand from living wood. This is the subject of much misunderstanding. Some say that the wood must be taken in such a way as to capture the dryad of the tree, but this is a kind of shorthand for something much more profound. Every plant has its own spirit, which embodies its character, its magical vibration, its lessons, and its complex connection within the Web of Life. Plants and trees must be approached as individuals and respected as living, spiritual entities. No two ash trees have the same personality.

To capture this is a difficult business. It is not as simple a matter as walking three times around a tree and saying, "Can I have a branch?", lopping one off, and leaving a coin in return. How many people know when they have gotten an answer? Is the plant even listening? You might as well buy a dried herb off the shelf in the local store, or pick up a dead twig from the garden. These instructions are based on folk magic, a distorted version of half-forgotten lore, a shadow of the true knowledge.

Kestrel, one of my old teachers, insisted that first of all a relationship must be established with the particular tree that you want to cut. Of necessity, this will be forged over a period of time; you must understand each other. Some trees are well-disposed toward humankind, some need to be persuaded, and some will never give you anything no matter what you do, and it would be dangerous to try. Based on Kestrel's teachings, the following describes how I took some oak wood one Midsummer morning:

Though it was still an hour to the rising of the Midsummer sun, it was light enough to see the dewy spider webs glinting like jewels in the hedgerows and strands of white mist rising from the water of the river, hanging in wisps among the reed, veiling the earth. I felt alone and outside of time as the rest of the world slept. With a great beating of wings a white swan took off from the bank, startling me—a good omen.

Conna, my fey friend, was waiting for me beneath the elder tree, heavily scented with its midsummer blossoms: the Great Elder Mother, mistress of deep magic, unpredictable, sometimes stern, sometimes fierce, and sometimes gentle. Today she smiled. Conna gestured that we should make haste, indicating the growing light; we must finish before dawn.

To enter the depths of the woodland we would have to pass by its Guardian, who protected its secrets from the unprepared. This was the first test. As I fought my way through the briars of the wild roses and thorns, I heard his hoof fall and the rise and fall of his breath. I felt a momentary panic, but his presence faded with a sigh. We had gained entry.

The paths were tangled and overgrown and it was a favorite game of the wood to mislead me and send me off in the wrong direction. Conna smiled and set off confidently, trotting off through the nettles and brambles that hampered and slowed me down. Finally I came into the presence of the Great Lord of the Forest, immeasurably old, tall, strong, and powerful. I felt suddenly overawed and dismayed at my impudence. I wondered how I had dared undertake this thing.

He looked down on me, a small and insignificant youngster, with patience, and even seemed amused. Then I felt Conna's hand on my shoulder, encouraging me. I was aware that the sun would soon rise and the time had come to act, if I dared. The Forest King's subjects clustered around him, ready to defend him from my knife. Sharp claws clutched at me, stinging, scratching, tearing my clothes and skin, and the battle heat was fierce as I fought my way through to stand at the foot of the Lord. Power radiated from him, the strength of his life force, the wisdom gained with the passage of many years. But I had won through and passed each test and he must submit.

Fearlessly he held out one of his limbs toward me even knowing the pain I intended to inflict upon him. With one clean blow I removed his limb, my own blood flowing from my battle wounds and mixing with his, exchanging some of my life force for his own as for a brief moment our spirits mingled and I understood.

His brave defenders now lay scattered and defeated on the woodland floor—crushed nettles and blackberry thorns.

I raised the pulsing, living oak bough I had captured to the newly risen solstice sun. Conna nodded and grinned briefly before disappearing into the trees, back to the realm of the wildfolk.

Making Your Wand

You should go out before dawn on Midsummer Day and seek your chosen tree as the sun rises. The wood should be virgin—that is, of one year's growth only—and the wand should be cut from the tree at a single stroke. It should measure from elbow to fingertip. If you wish, you can smooth and polish the wand with glass-paper, but do not varnish it. Make a small hollow in the end that you will hold in your hand, and insert of piece of cotton thread with a drop of your own blood into it, before sealing it with wax.

Consecrating the Wand

The wand is consecrated with incense of bay, cedar, frankincense, hazel, and pine, with the following words:

God and Goddess, deign to bless this wand, which I would consecrate and set aside. Let it obtain the necessary virtues for acts of beauty and love in the names of the Lord and Lady.

Pass it through the elements in the following manner. Push the tip into the earth, through the candle flame, into the dish of water, and through the air in the sign of the pentacle, and then say:

> *God and Goddess, I call upon you to bless this instrument, which I have prepared in your honor.*

Hold it high in the air and say:

> *Let blessing be.*

Woods for the Wand

The function of the wand largely depends on the wood from which it is made:

Alder—Support, foundation, magical beginnings, fire and water magic

Apple—An apple wand is used for love magic, for rituals designed to establish contact with the Otherworld, for initiation, and for fertility rituals

Ash—The ash is a great conductor of magical force, traditionally used for witches' broomsticks, druids' wands, and cunning men's staffs; the use of the ash wand connects the magician to all three realms, and when using an ash wand he or she acts within all three

Aspen—The aspen is used to invoke magical shields, for protection, and for healing

Bay—The bay tree is associated with the sun god and his powers of protection, healing, and divination; a bay wand may be used in all these rituals

Beech—The beech tree is associated with written knowledge; use a beech wand for spells and rituals concerning such knowledge, and in the consecration of written talismans

Birch—The birch is a tree of fertility, but is also a powerful magical force in rituals of purification and the banishment of negativity

Blackthorn—A blackthorn wand can be used for great good or great ill; it is a powerful magical protection, but also an instrument of cursing, used anciently to invoke the Wild Hunt to carry off the soul of an enemy

Bramble—Healing

Buckthorn—Healing

Cypress—Rites for the dead, crossing the gates of the underworld

Elder—Rites of the crone goddess, rites of Samhain and winter, fairy contact, healing, and summoning spirits

Elm—Rites of the Goddess, feminine magic

Hawthorn—Protection, invoking a psychic shield, fairy contact, the rite of Beltane, and Goddess magic

Hazel—A good general-purpose wand, some say this is the most efficacious of all wands; a hazel wand is sometimes called the *wishing rod*

Holly—Rites of male magic, warrior magic, protection from negative forces

Ivy—Binding magic, protection from psychic attack

Juniper—For warding off the evil eye, exorcism

Linden—Feminine power and rites of the Goddess

Maple—Handfastings, rituals of celebration

Mistletoe—Rites of healing, luck, and good fortune

Oak—Rites of protection, general-purpose magic, Midsummer, divination, fairy contact, Otherworld magic

Pine—Gaining knowledge, fire magic, illumination

Poplar—Divination

Rowan—Protection, divination

Service Tree—Protection, or as an all-purpose wand

Spindle Tree—Spinning and weaving magic, creating magic, Goddess magic

Whitebeam—Earth magic

Willow—Bardic magic, healing, Goddess magic, feminine magic, rebirth, purification

Yew—Initiation, funeral rites

Midsummer Spells

Sweethearts' Blossom Spell

Take a lily bulb and plant it in a clean pot that has never been used before. While you plant it, repeat the name of the one you love, and then say:

> *As this root grows*
> *And as this blossom blows,*
> *May her (his) heart be*
> *Turned unto me.*

Apple Spell to Keep a Lover

You will need the following:

    A lock of your lover's hair
    A lock of your own hair
    A large apple
    Red rose petals
    A pink ribbon

Hollow out the apple. Take the two locks of hair and knot them together, saying:

> *As I twist these locks of hair*
> *Binding together the life we share*
> *Loving together we shall be*
> *As I will, so mote it be.*

Place the locks inside the hollowed-out apple along with the red rose petals. Place the two apple halves back together and bind with the pink ribbon. Bury it in the earth, preferably at the foot of an apple tree. Should you wish to be rid of the lover at a future date, it will be necessary to dig up the apple and separate the locks of hair, which is difficult. This spell should not be performed unless you mean it and *not* without the permission of the lover—do so at your own peril.

Midsummer Candle Spell

For a general well-being and prosperity spell, take a yellow or gold candle and anoint it with marigold oil, saying:

> *In honor of the Lord and Lady on this Eve of St. John, grant me fruitfulness and profit of my planting and my work. In the name of the Lady and her Lord. So mote it be.*

Old Irish Pebble Spell

This spell is an old Irish custom. Walking around the Midsummer bonfire, state your requests (e.g., Cure my asthma. . . . Help me learn the ways of the Craft. . . . Let me discover my familiar, etc.) and cast in a pebble at the end of each prayer/ request.

Burning Away Negativity

Throw into the fire all things that represent things that have negative associations for you. You might take the opportunity to give up smoking, for example, by throwing a pack of cigarettes into the flames. Old magical tools and books that are no longer needed or that are broken can be disposed of in the Midsummer fire.

A Midsummer Horn

It is traditional to bang drums and blow horns during the festivities. The Irish made a glass horn by placing an inch or two of water in a glass bottle. This would be placed in the fire and hopefully snap off clean as it was heated. The sound of such a horn will carry for miles.

Oatmeal Lots

An old Welsh spell to ensure fertility and prosperity for the coming year involves preparing two types of cakes or buns, one of pale oatmeal, the other of dark meal.

Both types are split into four and placed in a bag. Everyone present has to pick out a piece. Those who pick out brown meal have to leap three times over the fire to ensure a plentiful harvest.

Baal Fire Ashes

The ashes of the Midsummer fire are lucky and should be taken home to be used in protective or healing amulets, or dug into the garden to ensure fertility. Ashes from the fire are placed in shoes to protect the wearer from bad luck, while a charred stick protects the home.

Torch Protection Spell

Carry a lighted torch or candle lantern (it must be some form of living flame, but be careful with it) all around the boundaries of your property, especially the garden where things are growing. This will encourage the crops and protect the whole property for the coming year.

Leaping the Fire

For luck and health in the coming year, it is traditional to leap over the bonfire. Wait until it has died down a little, as scorched robes are not part of the charm. If you do not have a bonfire, place three yellow or gold candles in the cauldron or dish in the center of the ritual space. These can be jumped over to fulfill the charm.

Flower Chaplets

It is the custom to wear chaplets of flowers, leaves, and herbs at Midsummer. These include the leaves of oak, birch, fennel, thyme, rosemary, rue, and fern, and the flowers of St. John's wort, lavender, orpine, sunflower, carnation, chamomile and daisy. The making of these is in itself a charm.

To construct a chaplet you will need a variety of the above flowers and herbs, some florist's wire and tape, and some gold and yellow ribbons. First, using the thicker wire, construct a circle that will fit comfortably on your head. Wrap the green florist's tape around it until it is completely covered. Now using fine wires you can begin to attach the flowers and leaves, with the following chant:

One for the Goddess, and one for the God
This one even, and this one odd
Rosemary, rue, and sweet orpine

Daisy, fern, and celandine
We tread the circle about and about
Dancing gaily tout a tout tout!
Thread the ring about and throughout
Laughing gaily tout a tout tout!
One for the Lady and one for her Lord
One for the sheath, then one for the sword!

Finish by wrapping the florist's tape over the exposed wires, and knotting on the ribbons so that they dangle at the back.

Threading the Needle

This is a traditional dance for Midsummer that requires quite a number of people to perform it effectively. Everyone should take hands and form a line, dancing along in the line to the music, following wherever the leader (usually the priestess) cares to take them. Then the leader begins to thread through the line, dragging the others after her. This is done by ducking under the arms of the others, who must not let go of each other's hands and break the line. Needless to say, this can all get very silly, and the dance usually collapses in laughter.

The dance is a fertility custom, and the connotations of "threading the needle" should be obvious.

Make Your Own Stone Circle

A stone circle is not simply a circle of stones. Nor is it, as you might think, set up in relation to the cardinal points. The stones mark the rising and setting of the sun at certain times of the year. Some, like Stonehenge, also mark the extent of the moon's wanderings in the sky. If you have enough space on your land—and the circle does not have to be massive—then you can begin to construct your very own "Stonehenge." Be warned: It will involve a lot of hard work and some days of getting up very early in the morning, and it will take a whole year.

First you will need to mark the point from which you will sight all your observations. This will be the center of the circle. Mark it with a peg. Attach a piece of string to it, the length of the required radius of the circle. Pull it taut and use it to mark the circumference of the circle with sand or salt. At dawn on each of the eight festivals (or just the solstices if you prefer), you will need to lie flat on the ground behind the peg and sight the place of the rising sun on the outer circumference. Mark the exact spot with a peg or stone. Mark the point of sunset with another stone.

After the space of a year, you will have the satisfaction of seeing the sun rise and set over your stones. This will be a potent place to hold rituals and perform other magical exercises, especially if the stones used are quartz-bearing rocks.

---

1. Horace, *Satires* 2:3.

2. Venetia Newall, "Midsummer Eve," *Man Myth and Magic* (periodical).

3. Though this now relates to the Christian Trinity, satisfying the Celtic appetite for triplets of all kinds, it was once thought to have been the Triple Goddess.

4. Nigel Pennick, *Rune Magic* (Wellingborough: Aquarian Books, 1992).

5. Ibid.

6. A word still used in Scotland to denote knowledge or understanding.

7. Good fairies start to come out around the vernal equinox, are very animated by Beltane, and are at the peak of their activities by Midsummer. By Halloween, most of the good fairies have disappeared from sight, and the bad fairies, such as goblins, rule the winter period.

8. W. B. Yeats, *Folk and Fairy Tales of the Irish Peasantry* (1888).

9. A. J. Huxley, *Man, Myth and Magic* (periodical).

10. Lady Augusta Gregory, *Visions and Beliefs of the West of Ireland* (Colin Smythe, 1920).

11. MS. Ashmole 1406, Bodleian Library.

12. A natural feature of the landscape that looks like a throne, or a rock outcrop associated with fairies.

13. Crofton Croker, *Fairy Legends and Traditions of the South of Ireland* (London: John Murray, 1827).

14. Lady Wilde, *Ancient Legends, Mystic Charms and Superstitions of Ireland* (London: Ward & Downey, 1887).

15. Kathryn Paulson, *The Complete Book of Magic and Witchcraft* (New York: Pentacle Press, 1970).

16. The Romans wore it to cure goiter.

Midsummer Herb Craft

As the Midsummer sun reaches the point of greatest power and light, it imbues herbs with special magical and healing properties. This is the most potent time for gathering herbs, especially sun-colored flowers such as St. John's wort. Other plants acquire strange properties; an elder cut on Midsummer Eve, for example, will bleed real blood, and fern seeds can confer the gift of invisibility if gathered at midnight. Anything round and rayed suggests the sun itself, including the rose and daisy.

A belief in the magical powers of herbs at Midsummer was common throughout Europe and the Middle East. At one time plants were hung up all over on St. John's Eve. In 1598 the historian John Stow wrote of the sight in London:

Every man's door was shaded with green birch, fennel, St. John's wort, orpin, white lilies, and the like, ornamented with garlands of beautiful flowers. They . . . had also lamps of glass with oil burning in them all night; and some of them hung out branches of iron, curiously wrought, containing hundreds of lamps lighted at once, which made a splendid appearance.[1]

Witches believe that plants gathered at the time of the summer solstice are endowed with distinct magical characteristics.

This is a fertile time of year when flowers bloom in abundance. In the Western Mystery Tradition it is counted as the time when the opening flower is fertilized, when the God impregnates the Goddess. For the Welsh it was sacred to the goddess Blodeuwedd, the Flower Bride, who was created by magic from nine types of flowers to marry the god Lleu Llaw Gyffes. The Celts made floral sacrifices at Midsummer. Well into the nineteenth century, people carried on this custom in Britain by placing flowers on the largest  stone on the farm. Protective plants were hung above the door and cattle stalls, including St. John's wort, rue, orpine, trefoil, rowan and red thread, vervain, and fennel.

If you gather your own herbal ingredients at Midsummer to use in magic, spells, and incense, you will be certain that they have been gathered in a reverent, magically empowered manner. When you come to mix the potion, cast the spell, or blend the incense, you will remember the atmosphere of the meadow, riverbank, or garden where you picked the herbs. You will remember the day, the season, and the enchanted feelings you had at the time.

Gathering Herbs for Magic

Make sure the herbs you collect are not growing near a busy road, as they will be polluted. Do not use iron or steel to cut them, as this earths their life force, and don't let them touch the ground after they've been picked, as this has the same effect. You should ask permission of the plant first, and state why you want its gifts. If you don't think you've received a reply, or are not sure, leave it alone. Only take a little of any one plant—don't strip it bare so that it will die. Place the plant matter in a clean paper, plastic, or fabric bag.

What nature provides is seasonal, and gathering ingredients can be a magical lesson in itself, attuning you to the turning of the year and teaching you about herb craft. It is helpful to gather produce on a dry day, as any dampness has a tendency to turn into mildew.

Drying Herbs

Any fresh herbs can be dried. They should be picked and tied in small bunches. Hang them in the kitchen or a well-ventilated shed to dry. As soon as they are dried out, they should be crumbled into jars and stored in a dark place—they might look decorative hanging up, but will soon become dusty and begin to deteriorate.

Special Uses for Herbs at Midsummer

The following herbs all take on special meaning at the summer solstice:

Alder *Alnus* **sp.**—The alder is widespread in Asia, Africa, the United States, and Europe, fringing streams, rivers, and lakes. Alder wood is oily and endures for a long time underwater, so it was once used to make bridges. The alder symbolizes the warm fire of the sun. Alder can be used in incenses for divination and scrying, and in incenses to invoke Bran, Herakles, Gwern, Apollo, Arthur, and Guinevere.

> **Alder Bark Magical Ink**
> 1 lb. alder bark
> 1 lb. iron sulfate
> 1 lb. gum arabic
> 1 gallon distilled water
>
> Boil the ingredients for four hours until the desired color and consistency are reached. If necessary add more alder bark and repeat the process. This ink can then be used for inscribing talismans and spells.

Angelica *Angelica* **sp.**—Angelica is a member of the parsley family and is probably a native of Europe. There are about thirty varieties. Angelica is invested with the power of the sun and light, the ability to cast off darkness and negativity. Use in incenses for Midsummer to celebrate the healing power of fire and the sun to overcome winter, decay, and negativity. Angelica was used in medieval Europe to deter evil spirits, especially at Midsummer when they were thought to roam freely. It is an important ingredient in incenses of healing, protection, cleansing, exorcism, and purification.

Angelica Lustral Water

Infuse two heads of angelica flowers in a large glass jar or ceramic jug of hot water. Strain the water from the flowers, being careful not to use any metal implements or containers. The resulting infusion can be used to purify the aura, the temple or sacred space, and magical tools, as well as houses and work places. Sprinkle it about your person, add some to your bath, or use a sprig of rosemary to sprinkle it about the temple or home.

Angelica Magical Oil

Loosely pack a jar with angelica leaves and fill with sunflower oil. Leave on a sunny windowsill for two weeks, giving it a good shake every day. Strain into a clean jar. For extra effectiveness the leaves should be gathered on Midsummer morning.

This oil can be used for protection. Smear a little around the edges of the doors and windows of your home, wear a little if you feel threatened, or use in a protection spell, such as the following:

Angelica Protection Spell

Angelica magical oil (see above)
1 blue candle
Protection incense (see incense recipes at the end of this chapter)
Matches

If you would like to protect your home, your family, a friend, or if you feel in need of magical protection yourself, you might like to use this spell. Set up your altar and place the blue candle in a holder. Meditate on what you need to be protected from. Take the oil and anoint the candle middle to bottom, then middle to top, saying:

By this candle's blessed light
Burning brightly in the night
By Midsummer's mighty power
Protect me rightly from this hour
By the Queen, the one in three
As I will, so mote it be.

Light the candle and visualize a globe of protective light surrounding first the candle, then the person or place you wish to protect. Allow the candle to burn down naturally.

Angelica Tea

> 1 tsp. cut angelica root
> 1 cup water

Put the root into the water and bring to a boil. Simmer for two minutes, then strain and drink with a little honey to sweeten if desired. This tea will stimulate the appetite and is an aid to digestion. It may be used externally to bathe tired eyes.

**N.B. Diabetics should not take angelica internally.*

Apple *Malus* **sp.**—The apple is a symbol of the sun. When an apple is cut in half it reveals a pentacle—the symbol of the goddess and the planet Venus, the Morning and Evening Star. Apple blossoms and wood are especially sacred to the goddess of love and may be used in spells and rituals of love and harmony. Apples may be used in incenses to invoke and honor the Goddess in her many aspects, including Aphrodite, Cerridwen, Diana, Eve, Flora, Godiva, the Hesperides, Iduna, Olwen, Titaea, Venus, the Mêliae (apple nymphs), Nehallenia, Inanna, Demeter, Iduna, Morgana, Pomona, and Nemesis. The apple also is sacred to the sun god, Apollo, Zeus, Herakles, Lugh, and Bel.

Ash *Fraxinus sp*.—Ash trees attract lightning in the summer months, the fertilizing power of the sky god, darting from the heavens to be transmitted to the belly of Mother Earth through the agency of the tree. This makes it an axis mundi, or World Tree, linking all the planes of existence. A magician may use an ash wand or staff as a portable axis mundi. To learn how to make a wand, consult chapter 4.

Ash shavings are used in incenses designed for astral travel and for connecting with a horse familiar, which carries the magician across the realms. The ash is a tree of the sun, and the bark and leaves can be used in sun incenses or to purify the aura and infuse it with the vitalizing, healing energy of the sun. At one time people ate ash buds at the Midsummer solstice to protect themselves from enchantment.

Basil *Ocimum sp*.—Basil, an herb of fire, is called the *Witch's Herb*, and throughout the ages witches have employed it in various forms of magic—for healing and revitalizing the body, in love spells, to invoke sky deities, and during initiation rites—when death and rebirth is promised.

Add basil to the food in the Midsummer feast.

Bay *Laurus nobilis*—The sweet bay is an evergreen tree naturalized around the Mediterranean. Bay is used in incenses or offerings to invoke sun gods and goddesses, and gods and goddesses of the dawn. It has the power to uncover secrets, as an herb of prophecy and divination. **Though large quantities of the vapor are dangerous,** small measures of bay leaves can be added to incenses utilized for trance work, divination, and prophecy. Tarot cards can be consecrated with bay incense.

As an herb of protection, bay has the power to banish negativity and darkness. Bay incense can be used for cleansing the temple and magical tools and to magically "seal" doorways and windows against negativity. Bay is used sparingly in incenses to invoke the gods of healing, the element of fire, the zodiac sign of Leo, and to invoke Adonis, Apollo, Aesculapius, Ceres, Cerridwen, Cupid, Daphne, Eros, Faunus, Ra, Vishnu, Mars, and Ares.

Birch *Betula sp.*—The European birch tree has a bright, white bark and is associated with the sun. Birch bark may be added to incenses of purification and protection, as well as incenses celebrating the passage of the sun.

In country ritual, leafy branches of birch were used at Midsummer to bedeck houses and even signposts throughout the villages. It forms the May and Midsummer maypole, sometimes called "the summer tree." This is bedecked with ribbons and erected on the green so that dancing may take place around it (for more on Midsummer customs, see chapter 2).

In the Nordic tradition the birch (*beorc, byarka,* or *berkana*) is a symbol of Mother Earth and represents the feminine powers of growth, healing, and the natural world. It may be used to honor the summer goddess in the form of incenses (bark), temple decorations (leafy twigs), and wands. It may be added to incenses for Otherworld travel, vision, and divination.

*N.B. The essential oil of birch is toxic when ingested.

Birch Leaf Tea
½ oz. fresh green leaves
1 pint boiling water

Infuse for ten minutes, then strain and drink. An infusion of birch leaves can help rheumatism and gout. The leaves have diuretic and antiseptic properties, but do not harm the kidneys.

Carnation *Dianthus sp.*—Carnations originally grew wild in the Mediterranean region. The Athenians gave them the name *dianthos*, meaning "flower of Zeus." In earlier times the carnation was known as the *gillyflower*. The common name derives from the word *coronation*, because they were used for decorative garlands at festivals and coronations, and as wreaths to celebrate betrothals and marriage. Carnation can be used in the handfasting incense and in incenses designed for joyful celebrations in general, where it will impart the energy of the sun. It can be added to sun incenses, fire incenses, and protection incenses, and used at the festival of Midsummer. In France there is still a Carnation Day on June 29 that is dedicated to St. Peter and St. Paul.

Cedar *Cedrus* sp.—True cedars belong to the genus *Cedrus* and are native to mountainous areas of North Africa and Asia. This fragrant wood has been used in incenses for millennia. It drives away ghosts and evil spirits and dispels negativity. It is associated with eternity and preservation from decay and corruption. It represents the continuation of the soul. Use to invoke the deities Amun Ra, Cernunnos, and Wotan.

Chamomile *Anthemis nobilis, Matricaria chamomilla*—Chamomiles are native to Europe, North Africa, and temperate Asia. They are sacred to the sun and sun gods, including the Egyptian Ra, the Celtic Cernunnos, and the Norse Baldur. Chamomile connects with the sun god's power of healing, regeneration, and protection. It may be used in incenses with these intentions or added to herbal talismans to give them a boost of the sun god's power. Chamomile is one of the sacred herbs of Midsummer and may used in the incense or simply thrown onto the festival fire as an offering.

*N.B. Ragweed allergy sufferers may want to avoid chamomile.

Chamomile Tea

> 2 tsps. dried flowers
> 1 cup boiling water

Pour the water over the herb and infuse for five to ten minutes. Strain and drink, sweetened with a little honey if desired. The tea is a sedative and is a useful treatment for stress and anxiety. Drink the tea after meals to relieve indigestion. Gargle with it for sore throats and use it as an eyewash for sore eyes. Chamomile is one of the safest herbs of all to use.

Magically, drink the tea to connect with the inner powers of healing and regeneration. It is useful for restoring the spirit and comforting the emotions after a trauma or upset.

Chamomile Magical Oil

Pack a clear glass jar with chamomile flowers, then top up with sunflower or olive oil. Leave on a sunny windowsill for two weeks, shaking daily. Strain into a clean jar. The oil can be used in healing spells, either for anointing the patient or a candle used in a candle magic spell, or as a healing massage oil. Inhale the oil to relieve stress, or rub into your neck to aid restful sleep.

Chamomile Sleep Pillow

> Two pieces of cloth, 9 inches square
> A needle and thread
> Dried chamomile flowers

> Place the two pieces of cloth right sides together and seam around three sides. Turn the right sides out and stuff the resulting sack with chamomile flowers. Close up the last side by handstitching it. Place this small pillow on top of your own to induce refreshing and restful sleep.

Cinnamon *Cinnamonum zeylanicum/Cinnamonum lauraceae*—Cinnamon is a tree that is native to Sri Lanka and China. In the East, it was burnt in temples to purify them. Used in incenses, cinnamon raises magical vibration and creates a peaceful energy. It is therefore useful for rituals of healing and divination. It is an herb of the sun and the element of fire, and may be used to invoke Aesculapius, Aphrodite, Helios, Ra, and Venus.

Daisy (English) *Bellis perennis*—The daisy is a hardy perennial that is native to Europe and Asia. Its central yellow boss with white petals arrayed around it was thought to resemble the sun. It is sacred to sun gods and goddesses and is associated with purity, innocence, and faithful love. The daisy is sacred to the Baltic sun goddess Saule. Daisies picked between noon and one o'clock on Midsummer day have special magical qualities. They bring success in any venture when they are dried and carried.

The name *bellis* comes from the Latin *bellus*, which means "pretty." In classical myth, the daisy was created when the watermeadow nymph Belidis changed herself into a daisy to avoid the amorous attentions of the orchard god Vertumnus. Others have associated the derivation of the name with the Celtic god Belenos. The English name *daisy* comes from the Anglo-Saxon *daeges eage*, meaning "day's eye," and refers to the flower opening its petals during daylight hours and closing them at night.

Dill *Anethum graveolens*—Dill is an aromatic, upright, annual herb native to the eastern Mediterranean, India, Iran, Russia, and western Asia. It was known as one of the St. John's Eve herbs and was valued as a protection against witchcraft. Use as incense to clear your mind and strengthen your personal focus. It can be added to incense for protection and for cleansing the sacred space. To witches, dill is a sacred herb of Midsummer and can be used in the incense, cast on the bonfire, or used in the ritual cup.

Dill Love Bath (for men)

To attract women, add a small handful of dill seeds to your bath and soak yourself in the warm water for at least twenty minutes. When you go out to your party or nightclub, you should be irresistible.

Dill Protection Talisman

This is a very simple spell and needs no magical tools or words. The seed heads of dill hung in the home bring protection to those who live there. Keep some dill in the home to bring a feeling of well-being to guests and bestow blessings on the occupier.

Dill Love Cup

1 cup red wine
1 tsp. dill seeds

Put the wine in a saucepan and add the dill seeds. Warm the wine gently for five minutes, but do not boil. Strain and pour into a goblet and share with the one you love. Dill seeds infused in wine are considered to be an aphrodisiac, and magicians traditionally used dill in their love spells. This drink also makes a good loving cup for the couple at a handfasting.

Dill Infusion

Add a sprig of dill herb to a cup of boiling water and infuse for ten minutes. The resulting infusion may be added to water to cleanse the sacred space or to the ritual cleansing bath.

Dill Magical Oil

Pack a clean glass jar with dill herb. Fill the jar with sunflower oil and leave on a sunny windowsill for two weeks. Strain the oil into a clean jar. Stopper tightly and label. Dill oil can be used to seal protective talismans and doorways and windows against negative influences—smear the oil around the frames.

Elder *Sambucus nigra*—Elder is the name of a group of thirty species of small trees that grow in temperate areas in the Northern Hemisphere. It is said that where the elder grows, the Goddess is not far away. The elder has several stations throughout the year, and its character changes at each. The sweet blossom can be collected in June and makes a good fixative for herbal incenses. The leaves should be gathered on Midsummer morning to add to healing incenses. Add the blossom to Coamhain incense and to incenses to invoke dryads and fairies.

N.B. Elder bark, roots, leaves, and unripe berries are toxic if ingested.

Midsummer Elderflower Love Charm

A love charm can be made by putting elderflowers into a tankard of ale to be shared by a man and woman. They will then be married within the year.

Elderflower Tea

1 cup boiling water

2 tsps. fresh or dried elderflower blossoms

Infuse together for ten minutes. Drink three times daily to lower the temperature and to treat colds accompanied by fever and flu. This may also be of benefit in cases of hayfever, bronchitis, sinusitis, and other catarrhal inflammations of the upper respiratory tract.

Elder Leaf Salve

6 parts petroleum jelly

3 parts fresh elder leaves

Heat together until the leaves go crisp. Strain into a glass jar. The leaves may be made into an ointment for treating bruises and sprains.

Elderflower Gargle for Sore Throats

2 tsps. elderflowers

2 tsps. sage leaves

1 cup boiling vinegar

1 tsp. honey

Infuse the leaves in the hot vinegar for fifteen minutes. Strain and add the honey. Cool and use as a gargle.

Fennel—Fennel was held in high esteem by the Romans and was one of the nine sacred herbs of the Anglo-Saxons. During the Middle Ages fennel was hung over the door on Midsummer Eve, as it was believed to keep away evil spirits. It is one of the witch's sacred aromatic herbs of Midsummer, used as incense or thrown on the bonfire. It has a long association with the sun and fire. In Greek mythology the titan Prometheus used a hollow fennel stem to steal fire from the sun and bring it to humankind. Greek islanders still carry lighted coals around in the pith of giant fennel.

N.B. Ingesting fennel oil may cause vomiting or seizures.

Fennel Tea

1 tsp. crushed fennel seeds

1 cup water

Boil together for ten minutes, strain, and drink, sweetened with a little honey if desired. An infusion of the crushed seeds is a well-known remedy for digestive complaints such as flatulence, colic, loss of appetite, and stomach pains. It stimulates the appetite and aids digestion. The infusion will increase the flow of milk in nursing mothers. Make a compress of the infusion to treat blepharitis (inflammation of the eyelids) or tired eyes.

N.B. Do not give tea sweetened with honey to children one year of age or younger—the honey can cause botulism.

Fern—Fern is the common name for any spore-producing plant of the phylum *Polypodiophyta*. It is associated with sun gods and goddesses, and gods and goddesses of the dawn, such as Daphne. It is also sacred to the Great Goddess and the sky gods of thunder, lightning, and Midsummer. At the turning of Midsummer and Midwinter, it allows access into the Otherworld and contact with its inhabitants, the Sidhe and Wildfolk. It was sacred to the Baltic sun goddess Saule, who appeared on the horizon at Midsummer, wreathed in apple blossom and red fern blossom (i.e., red clouds). Use fern in incenses at Midsummer to protect the household and for divination purposes.

N.B. Many varieties of fern plants are toxic if ingested.

Collecting Magical Fernseed

At Midsummer the magical fernseed is collected. At midnight it glows with a magic light. The plant must not be touched directly, but bent with a forked hazel stick over a pewter plate. The seed is so tiny that it is almost invisible, and therefore was thought to convey invisibility to its possessor. In Lancashire (northern England) it was held that fernseed collected on the family Bible conveyed invisibility.

The Hand of Glory[2]

Lucky hands made of the rootstock of the male fern trimmed to a likeness of thumbs and fingers were smoked in the Midsummer fires and hung up for protection in houses and farms. Such hands are said to reveal hidden treasure buried within the earth, glowing with a blue flame.

Flax *Linaceae sp*.—The flax family is a member of the order *Linales,* the most ancient class of flowering plants native to almost all tropical and temperate regions. Flax thread is intimately connected to the life maze and to the Web of Life. Flax may be used in incense to consecrate the ritual wheel or sun/moon disc or zodiac symbol. Flax may be thrown onto the fire at Midsummer. The Lapps offered flax on the altars of the sun goddess, because many sun deities are associated with spinning, whether spinning the cosmos itself or spinning sunbeams.

Flax Love Spell

Linen thread, at least 4 feet long

An image of the one you love

7 pink candles

Matches

Take a length of linen thread and tie one end around an image of the one you love. This might be a photograph or a wax puppet fashioned into a likeness (it doesn't have to be accurate) of him or her. Light the seven pink candles and seat yourself the length of the thread away from the image. Slowly draw it toward you by pulling the thread while chanting the following:

Dance the circle dance of dreaming,
Lonely by the crystal sea,
Spin the web of mist and moonlight
Come, beloved, and follow me.

Chant the chant of souls entwining
Round and through the scared fire,
Drink from wells of mist and moonshine
Lover, come to love's desire.

Dream the dream of solemn passion
Through the star encrusted night,
Weave the web of mist and moonfire
Loved one, know all love's delight.

Hear the tides, the heaving waters,
Somber on the crystal sand
Hear the chant of longing, waiting,
Come, fulfill at love's demand.

Seek and love my waiting body,
Waiting nightly by the sea,
Tread the path of mist and moonlight,
Lover, come beloved, to me.[3]

Linseed Oil—The oil extracted from the seeds of flax is known as linseed oil. It has soothing and lubricating properties and can be used to treat tonsillitis, sore throats, coughs, colds, and constipation. The oil is sometimes given as a laxative, and mixed with honey it is used as a cosmetic to treat pimples.

N.B. Buy your linseed oil ready-made, as the immature seeds can be poisonous.

Frankincense *Boswellia thurifera/Boswellia carteri*—Frankincense is a gum resin obtained from the *Boswellia thurifera* tree. The tree is native to the Middle East and Somalia. It is widely used as an important ingredient of incense. It cleanses, purifies, consecrates, and raises vibrations. As such it may be added to most incenses, but is particularly useful in purification and meditation incenses. The fragrance concentrates the mind, lifts melancholy, and drives away negativity. It is beneficial for those who dwell too much in the past and for those who find physical contact difficult. Its perfume releases vibrations that lift the spirits of all those in the vicinity.

Frankincense is associated with sun gods and may be used in all rituals involving the sun. Frankincense is also associated with moon goddesses and may be used during moon rituals. Use also to invoke the deities Adonis, Aphrodite, Apollo, Bel, Demeter, Hades, Helios, Jehovah, Jesus, moon goddesses, Pluto, Ra, other sun gods, Venus, Vishnu, Vulcan, and Yama.

Gorse *Ulex eurpaeus*—Furze, or gorse, is native to Europe and is widely cultivated. The sun and the element of fire rule it. Use to invoke Jupiter, Onniona, spring goddesses, sun gods, and Thor. It was burned at Midsummer and blazing branches were carried around the herd to bring good health to the cows and good luck for the rest of the year. In some parts of the British Isles the Midsummer fire was lit with a branch of gorse.

Gorse Flower Tea
> 4 large spoonfuls gorse flowers
> 1 pint boiling water
> Honey or brown sugar to taste

Crush the flowers slightly, pour on the water, and infuse for ten to twelve minutes. Strain and sweeten if desired. A tea of the fresh flowers is a diuretic.

Gorse is a herb that brings hope and positivity. It can be used to reconnect with the soul. It is useful for people who are depressed, by helping them find their true path and the energy and personal strength needed to take positive action.

Hazel *Corylus avellana*—Hazel is the common name applied to trees and shrubs of the genus *Corylus,* found throughout the temperate regions of North America and Eurasia. A branch of hazel cut at Midsummer Eve will guide you to hidden treasure. It must be cut at night by walking backward with both hands between your legs. Hazel wood is sacred to the fairy Wildfolk and to the god Lugh. Add to incense designed to invoke sun and moon deities.

Hazel Divination Rod

This is best cut at Midsummer. Look for a forked twig of hazel growing strongly on a healthy plant. Cut it off as cleanly as possible, with both legs of the fork of equal length. To use the divining rod, grasp the two forks loosely in your hands. The rod is traditionally used for finding underground streams and springs. When it crosses water, the wand will dip and twist in the hands of the diviner.

Heather *Calluna vulgaris*—Heather is an evergreen shrub belonging to the family *Ericaceae,* found throughout western Europe and in parts of North America. It is sacred to the goddess of Midsummer, who was often designated as queen bee, as bees love to drink from heather flowers. The goddess Cybele was the queen bee for whom her priests castrated themselves to become her drones. In legend, Cybele imprisoned Attis in heather at Midsummer.

The honeybee, which orientates itself on its journey from the heather to the hive in relation to the position and angle to the sun, was regarded by the Celts as a messenger traveling the path of the sunlight to the spirit world.

Heather Tea

2 tsps. dried heather flowers

1 cup boiling water

Pour the boiling water over the herb and infuse for ten minutes. Strain and drink. Heather blossoms make a tonic tea. In northern parts of Britain, people often added the tips of flowering shoots to herbal drinks and beer to purify the blood. When used externally the infusion benefits the complexion and rids it of freckles.

Honeysuckle *Lonicera caprifolium*—The family *Caprifoliaceae* contains about 400 species and occurs mainly in the North Temperate Zone. Add the flowers to Midsummer incenses. Honeysuckle can be used in incenses to invoke or honor the god Pan and to connect with goat and bee totems and the fairy folk. Add to incense of the goddess Cerridwen.

Honeysuckle Oil

Pack a clean glass jar with honeysuckle flowers and sunflower oil and leave on a sunny windowsill for two weeks. Strain off the oil, add it to a fresh batch of flowers, and leave again for two weeks. Repeat the process until the oil is pleasantly scented.

The resulting oil can be used in rites of Pan, the goddess Cerridwen, and the Flower Bride. Use to anoint the coveners as they enter the circle, or anoint the candles and tools with it.

The warmed oil can be used for treating chilblains and to improve the circulation. Rub it into the hands and feet.

Lavender *Lavendula officinalis*—Lavender is the name given to twenty-eight species of the genus *Lavandula,* native to the Mediterranean region. Use in incenses for the planet Mercury, the element of air, and to invoke the deities Cernunnos, Circe, Hecate, Medea, Saturn, and serpent goddesses. Lavender purifies, heals, and cleanses. Add to incenses for calm meditation and to bring peace and harmony in the home or at difficult discussions and meetings. Add to Midsummer incense.

To See Midsummer Fairies

Go to a natural or wild place, a fairy mound, or any other spot known to be haunted by the fairy folk. Carry with you a sprig of lavender and inhale the scent. On old charm says that this will help you see the Little People.

Lavender Posy for Handfast Lovers

    7 sprigs lavender flowers

    1 pink ribbon

    1 sprig white heather

Bind the flowers together and tie with the pink ribbon. Lavender posies were often given to newly married couples to bring them luck for the future.

Lavender Peace Spell

To bring peace and harmony to your home, crumble some dried lavender flowers in your hands, saying:

> *As I crush these lavender flowers*
> *Heralds of love and peaceful hours*
> *Grant this home true harmony*
> *By the Queen, the one in three*
> *As I will, so mote it be.*

Sprinkle the lavender about your home.

Lavender Infusion

    1 tsp. lavender flowers

    1 cup boiling water

Infuse together for ten minutes, strain and drink. An infusion of the flowers is effective in the treatment of headaches, depression, insomnia, indigestion, stress, dizziness, nausea, flatulence, and colic. It can be used as a mouthwash for oral thrush and bad breath, as a general tonic, and for respiratory problems, tonsillitis, colds, flu, and high temperatures.

Lemon Balm *Melissa officinalis*—Lemon balm is a hardy, herbaceous perennial native to southern Europe. Use in incenses of the moon, the element of water, the zodiac sign of Cancer, and to invoke the deities Artemis, Diana, and other moon goddesses. Add to healing incenses, particularly to heal emotional problems. Lemon balm has a reputation as a healing and refreshing plant. In southern Europe it is called "heart's delight" and "the elixir of life."

    The regular drinking of lemon balm tea was said to increase the life span. Llewelyn, prince of Glamorgan during the thirteenth century, was said to have drunk the tea daily and he lived to be 108 years old. It was recommended to students in the sixteenth century to use lemon balm, as it cleared the mind, sharpened the understanding, and increased the memory. The bruised leaves or juice of leaves or stems can be applied directly onto insect bites, pimples, boils, and sores.

Lemon Balm Tea

> 1 handful lemon balm leaves
> 1 cup boiling water

Infuse for ten to fifteen minutes and drink a cup in the morning and evening. The tea can be used to provide relief from catarrh and headaches, to lower the temperature, and to ease tension. The balm is useful for indigestion caused by anxiety or depression, and it also works to relieve stress and depression. An infusion of balm leaves can be used as a facial steam or as a rinse for greasy hair.

Lemon Balm Bath

> 1 handful fresh lemon balm leaves
> 1 cup boiling water

Infuse for fifteen minutes, strain, and add the infusion to the bath to soothe and refresh both the mind and body.

Mallow *Malva sylvestris*—In Ireland the young people gathered sprigs of mallow on Midsummer Eve. It was considered to be a protection from some of the more dangerous spirits at large on this night. They would then touch their relatives and friends with the leaves, and throw the leaves onto the bonfire.

Mallow Infusion

> 1 handful fresh mallow petals
> 1 cup boiling water

Pour the boiling water over the flowers and infuse for fifteen minutes. Both the common and the musk mallow have similar properties. They both contain mucilage, which makes them useful for the treatment of coughs.

Mallow Ointment

Gently simmer fresh mallow leaves in petroleum jelly for ten to fifteen minutes. Strain into clean jars. This can be applied to bruises, wounds, cuts, stings, and burns. It also serves as a protective salve at Midsummer.

Marigold *Calendula officinalis*—Marigold is a hardy, annual herb native to central and southern Europe and Asia. Use it in incenses dedicated to the sun, the element of fire, the zodiac sign of Leo, and to invoke sun gods. Marigold is an herb of healing and protection. It can also be added to incenses for prophetic dreams, love, and divination, and used to consecrate divinatory tools such as crystal balls.

The name of this plant comes from the Latin *calends,* or *kalendae,* the word for the first day of each month and the origin of our "calendar." In ancient Rome the calendula was said to be in bloom on each "calend" throughout the year. The specific name *officinalis* shows that it was included on the official list of herbal medicines. In ancient Egypt it was used as a rejuvenating herb, while the Persians and Greeks used it for cooking, and the Hindus to decorate their altars and temples.

At Midsummer garlands of marigold flowers hung on doors prevent evil from entering. Marigold petals are also scattered on the floor under the bed to offer protection to sleepers.

Marigold Attraction Bath (for women)

To ensure the respect and admiration of everyone, add a small handful of marigold petals to your bath water.

Summerland Blessing

Marigolds planted on graves bless the departed soul. This is a good time of year to remember those who have gone from this life into the realms that we call the *Summerland.*

Marigold Tea

Marigold flower heads, preferably the double sort, are used medicinally. Marigold has antifungal properties and can be used both internally and externally. Infuse half a handful of petals in a cup of boiling water for ten minutes.

Calendula flower infusion, applied externally, is good for the treatment of burns, varicose veins, bruises, gum inflammations, and skin rashes. Taken internally as a tea, it can help menstrual cramps and aid digestion. Drink two cups, warm, per day when needed. A calendula mouthwash is particularly good after tooth extraction.

Marigold Salve
> Butter
> Marigold juice (extracted from the leaves using a mortar and pestle or
>   juice extractor)

Blend the juice and butter thoroughly, stirring in as much juice as the butter will take without becoming too liquid. Store in glass jars in a cool place and use as required. An ointment can be used for cracked skin, cuts, chilblains, catarrh, sunburn, acne, tired feet, hemorrhoids, and inflammations.

Infused Marigold Oil

Infusing the flower petals in a good vegetable oil, preferably sunflower oil, for three weeks makes a useful oil. This can then be used for healing burns, rashes and skin complaints, or magically for anointing candles, the tools of divination, and participants in solar rituals.

Marjoram *Origanum vulgare*—Marjoram is a member of the mint family and is native to North Africa and Asia. Add to incense dedicated to the deities Aphrodite, Jupiter, Osiris, Thor, Venus, or Hera. It is an herb of protection that repels negativity and fosters happiness. It is sacred to the goddess of love and may be used to invoke her in all her aspects. It is also used in love incenses and at weddings and handfastings. The Greeks believed that Aphrodite created marjoram as a symbol of happiness and that its scent came from its touch. They planted it on graves to give peace to the departed soul. Both the Greeks and the Romans used it to make garlands to crown newly married couples. Marjoram was an ingredient in fourteenth-century love potions. The plant has a reputation for healing grief, both in the human and animal kingdoms.

Marjoram Home Protection Charm
> 1 piece of white cloth
> 1 red ribbon
> Dried marjoram
> A few drops lemon balm oil

Place the dried marjoram on the white cloth and sprinkle with the lemon balm oil, saying:

> *By the goddess of love and happiness*
> *This herbal charm my home will bless*
> *Keeping us safe from evil powers*
> *All by the strength of these little flowers!*

Bind up the cloth with the red thread and hang it near the door where most people enter and leave. Placing marjoram around the house ensures happiness and acts as a protection against evil. It can also be grown in the garden as a protection.

Marjoram Gargle for Sore Throats

A mouthwash or gargle may be made by infusing two tablespoons of the herb in one pint of water for ten minutes. Use as needed for oral thrush and mouth infections.

Marjoram Soothing Bath

Add a handful of fresh or half a handful of dried marjoram to your bath water to provide a relaxing soak.

Marjoram Infusion

   1 cup boiling water
   2 tsps. marjoram

Pour the boiling water over the herb and infuse for fifteen minutes. Drink up to three times a day for no more than ten days. Use for colds, tension headaches and "poor nerves," coughs, whooping cough, flu, exhaustion, menstrual cramps, nervous headaches, and irritability. The tea may prevent seasickness. A weaker tea will soothe the nerves and relieve insomnia.

Used externally, the infusion may be used on infected cuts and wounds, swellings, bites and stings, and the symptoms of hayfever. Inhaling the steam from the infusing leaves aids tonsillitis, coughs, asthma, and bronchitis.

N.B. Do not use during pregnancy.

Meadowsweet *Filipendula ulmaria/Spiraea ulmaria*—Meadowsweet is a member of the rose family native to Europe, temperate Asia, and eastern North America. The generic name, *spiraea,* is the root word for *aspirin,* and meadowsweet has long been used for pain relief and the treatment of fevers.

Meadowsweet was one of the three most sacred herbs of the druids (the others were watermint and vervain). The druids are believed to have made use of the plant's anodyne qualities. It is sometimes known as "Queen of the Meadows," which was one of the titles of the Celtic goddess Blodeuwedd ("flower-face"). It is also sacred to the Celtic goddesses Aine and Gwena, and the Roman love goddess Venus.

The folk name of *bridewort* became popular because it was often used in bridal garlands and posies for bridesmaids. It was also frequently strewn in the church, on the path to the church, and in the home of the newlywed couples. It flowers from June through September, and these were the most popular months for marriages in druidic times. Use the flowers in incenses for love, marriage and handfasting, and fertility.

Meadowsweet can be used to scent robes and altar cloths. Place the flowers in chests and drawers to dedicate the clothes to the Goddess.

Meadowsweet Charm to Detect a Thief

Meadowsweet is believed to help detect a thief. When placed on water it will sink if the thief is a man and float if a woman.

Meadowsweet Attraction Oil (for women)

Loosely fill a jar with meadowsweet flowers and add enough vegetable oil to cover them. Leave in a warm place and shake daily for two weeks. Strain and bottle. Brides on their wedding night traditionally used this oil. Dab a little behind your ears, at your wrists, and behind your knees to make yourself irresistible.

Meadowsweet Tea

2 tsps. dried aerial parts of the herb

1 cup boiling water

Infuse for ten minutes. The infusion may be used to treat heartburn, acid stomachs, gastritis, diarrhea, fevers, rheumatism, gout, flu, bladder complaints, insomnia, and as a painkiller.

Meadowsweet Beauty Wash

Pick meadowsweet flowers on Midsummer morning with the dew still on them. Place the flowers in rainwater or distilled water and soak for twenty-four hours. Wash your face with the water to preserve your beauty forever.

Oak *Quercus robur*—There are more than 600 species of oaks, all of which grow naturally only in the Northern Hemisphere. The primary power plant of the summer solstice is the oak. In ogham the oak is *duir*, meaning "door" in Gaelic. The word for *door* and *oak*, and perhaps *druid*, come from the same root in many European languages. The oak flowers at Midsummer and marks the door opening on one side to the waxing year and on the other side to the waning year. Oak was the most sacred tree of the druids and stood for an axis mundi, and was the doorway to knowledge. Oak wood constituted the sacred fires of Midsummer. The flowers and wood are used at Coamhain. Use to invoke the deities Allah, Arianrhod, Artemis, Balder, Blodeuwedd, Brighid, Ceirddylad, Cernunnos, Cerridwen, Cybele, The Dagda, Dianus, Donar, Dryads, Erato, the Erinyes, Hades, Hecate, Hercules, Herne, Horus, Indra, Janicot, Janus, Jehovah, Jupiter, Kirke, Llyr, Nephthys, Odin, Pan, Pluto, Rhea, Tannus, Taran, Thor, Ukho, Vishnu, Zeus, Athene, Mars, Ares, and Ukko.

Druid's Oak Flower Tonic

2 tsps. oak flower buds
1 cup boiling water

Infuse together for five to ten minutes, strain and drink. When the oak flowered, around the time of the midsummer solstice, the druids made an infusion from the flower buds as an internal cleanser for the body.

Druid Midsummer Purification

The druids used pools of rainwater and dew found in the hollows of oak as a ritual cleanser for the Midsummer rites. If you are lucky enough to find such little pools of water, you might do the same to make a truly magical start to Midsummer Day.

Gathering Oak on Midsummer Day

This is the best time to gather oak for magical purposes, but when gathering wood, leaves, or acorns of the oak, it is lucky to feed the tree by pouring a libation of wine on the roots. Acorns are best gathered by day, and the leaves and branches by night.

Oak Bark Tea

Place one handful of oak bark in one cup of water. Simmer for ten minutes, strain, and drink up to three cups a day. Oaks are well-known for their astringent qualities. The infusion can be used externally in the treatment of hemorrhoids or as a gargle for sore throats. Oak bark tea may be used internally and externally to shrink varicose veins and as a wash for sores and skin irritations. It can also be used as a hair rinse to prevent dandruff.

N.B. Inner oak bark contains tannic acid, which is potentially toxic.

Orpine—Orpine is a purple-flowered stonecrop (*Sedum*) known as *Midsummer Men*. Orpine is the French word for *stonecrop*. The plant is also called "live long" as it will live for months after it is cut, if only it is sprinkled with a little water. It was set in pots on Midsummer Eve and hung up in the house as a form of love divination. If the leaves bent to the right this signified that a lover was faithful, but if to the left the "true love's heart was cold and faithless."[4] If two slips are stuck together in a crack and lean together, the omen is good for a relationship.

Reed *Phragmites communis*—The reed is found growing in marshes, at water edges, and in moist woodland in almost all countries of the temperate and warm regions. In myth the reed bed was seen as the entrance to the underworld from which the sun was reborn. Because reeds are filled with air—or spirit—reeds are associated with the speaking of the spirits. They are a symbol of royalty and sun gods, employed as scepters. Use to honor the deities Lugh, Pan, fairies, Taliesin, Unkulunkulu, Osiris, Inanna, Isis, Horus, Cybele, Attis, Hermes, Faunus, and Ra. Reed may be added to the Midsummer incense, and traditionally reed arrows are fired at the rising sun to encourage it.

Rose *Rosa* sp.—The rose is a symbol both of the sun and the Goddess. Use to honor and invoke the deities Adonis, Aphrodite, Bacchus, Blodeuwedd, Christ, Cupid, Demeter, Eros, Flora, Freya, Hathor, Hulda, Hymen, Isis, Nike, Venus, Vishnu, Bacchus, Flora, Hymen, the Mothers, Saule, Inanna, Ishtar, Artemis, Kubaba, Ninsianna, Dionysus, Harpocrates (Horus), and Aurora. Roses are symbolic of rebirth and resurrection. Burn rose petals to change your luck. The white rose represents purity, perfection, innocence, virginity, and  the Maiden Goddess, while the red rose is earthly passion and fertility, the Mother Goddess. Add rose petals to incense for spells and rituals of love, passion, sexuality and sensuality, seduction and marriage, the Great Rite, and handfasting.

West Country Rose Charm

Pick a rose on Midsummer morning and put it away wrapped in a piece of white paper. It will not fade. Wear it at the festival of Midwinter and your true love will reveal himself by taking it from you.

Rose Petal Tea

1 handful red rose petals

1 cup boiling water

Infuse for five to ten minutes. Strain and sweeten with honey if desired. This makes a calming drink or may be used externally to treat conjunctivitis or as an antiseptic tonic for the skin. It is especially useful for inflamed and sensitive skins.

Rose Consecration Water for Robes

2 pints rose water (available commercially)

1 tbsp. fresh lavender flowers

2 tbsps. orris root

4 drops clove essential oil

Place in a large glass jar and leave on a sunny windowsill for fourteen days. Strain into a clean jar and keep tightly stoppered. Add a teaspoonful to the final rinse water of your magical robes.

Rosemary *Rosemarinus officinalis*—Ruled by the sun and the element of fire, rosemary is a hardy perennial native to the Mediterranean region. It helps the mind and the memory, so use in incenses designed to help you concentrate or meditate. Use also for healing, marriage, births, funerals and memorial services, for protection and to dispel negativity and evil, to keep a lover faithful, for love spells, and for spells designed to retain youth. The fairy folk are particularly fond of rosemary, and the incense attracts them.

Rosemary is also considered to be an herb of love. In some places rosemary is a wedding herb, and all guests are greeted with a branch of rosemary wrapped in gold wire or foil and ribbons. Sometimes it was used as a garland for brides, even for queens. In the language of flowers, rosemary is the symbol of fidelity, love, remembrance, and friendship.

A piece of rosemary wood cut on Midsummer morning is said to preserve youthful looks.

Rosemary Spell to Keep a Lover Faithful

Gather rosemary leaves on Midsummer Day and dry them. On the first day of the waxing moon, powder the leaves and place them in a jar with a rose quartz crystal. At the full moon sprinkle the powdered rosemary under the bed you share with your lover.

Old Rosemary Love Spell

Tap the wedding ring finger of your intended three times with a sprig of rosemary. You will soon be married.

Rosemary Tea

1 cup boiling water
2 tsps. dried rosemary

Pour the boiling water over the herb, cover, and infuse for ten to fifteen minutes. Drink up to three times a day for no more than ten days. The infusion can be used for the treatment of depression, insomnia, anxiety, nervous migraines, rheumatic pain, and aching joints. The tea can be drunk daily as a tonic. It can also be used as an antiseptic gargle or mouthwash.

Externally it can be used to heal wounds, bruises, strains, and bumps. It stimulates the circulation and eases pain because it increases the blood supply to the area where it is applied.

Rosemary tea may be drunk to restore psychic energies after depletion and to strengthen the aura. The tea helps clear the mind and improve the memory if drunk just before a ritual.

Rosemary is a cleansing herb and repels negativity. It may be used in washes to purify the temple or working area and magical tools. It can be used in the ritual bath to purify the person.

A Little Sprig of Rosemary

A sprig of rosemary may be used as a sprinkler for casting lustral water about the temple or coveners. A sprig may be hung in the home to keep the atmosphere pure.

Rosemary Handfast Charm

To celebrate a handfasting, prepare a sprig of rosemary tied with a red ribbon for each guest. This is a lucky charm and will remind them of the day.

Rowan *Sorbus aucuparia*—Rowans are a group of trees or shrubs that grow in the Northern Hemisphere, mainly in high places. Rowan is associated with witchcraft, protection, divination, and the dead. The berries are marked with the sign of the pentagram, the sign of protection. The berries and leaves can be dried and burned as an incense to invoke spirits, familiars, spirit guides, and elementals to ask for their help when seeking visions, particularly at Samhain. The berries can also be used in incense to banish undesirable entities and thought forms.

Witchwand

Another name for rowan is *witchwand*, as divining rods for metal are made from rowan. Find a rowan tree or shrub where a forked branch is growing strongly. On Midsummer morning cut it off cleanly, making sure the two forks are of equal length. Grasp the two forks loosely in your hands. They will twitch and twist when you pass over buried metal, though this may take some practice.

Rowan Cross Protective Charm

As a protective charm, two twigs of rowan should be gathered, without use of a knife, and bound together with red thread to form an equal-armed cross, saying:

Rowan tree and red thread
Leave all wickedness in dread.

These may be hung up indoors or placed on the altar.

Rue *Ruta graveolens*—Rue is a hardy evergreen shrub native to southern Europe. It is an important herb for encouraging inner vision and clairvoyance, particularly for artistic people. It banishes negative energies and may be used in exorcism and purification incenses. The sun and the element of fire rule it. Use to invoke the deities Aradia, Diana, Hermes, Horus, Mars, Menthu, Mercury, and Odysseus.

Rue is often associated with witchcraft, used by and against witches. During the Middle Ages it was considered to be a protection against witchcraft and sorcery. It was hung in cattle sheds to protect the animals from incantations, disease, and insects. It was such an important herb in Italy that silver replicas of it were worn as amulets against the evil eye.

N.B. Fresh rue may be a skin irritant or cause an allergic reaction.

To Empower a Crystal Ball

For a magic potion that will empower your crystal ball or scrying glass, collect a bunch of rue from the garden, and dew from the Midsummer dawn. Crush the rue with a mortar and pestle and add nine drops of dew, saying:

Now sprinkle I the juice of rue,
With nine drops of morning dew
Glistening sun tears captured here
Let past seem present, let far seem near
Reveal what seers and witches see
As I will, so mote it be.

Rub the leaves and dew over the crystal ball or glass and leave for a while to absorb the power of the herbs and the Midsummer sunlight. Then wash the crystal and polish it with a clean, white cloth.

St. John's Wort *Hypericum perforatum*—St. John's wort is a hardy perennial herb native to Europe and western Asia. It is one of the many herbs that gain special powers at Midsummer, when it should be collected for magical purposes. The golden flowers are associated with the sun and the flames of the Midsummer fires. The Irish called it "life-renewer" (*beathnua*) and the Welsh "the blessed one's leaf" (*dail y fendigaid*). Medieval herbalists considered it the golden herb that "shines like the sun in the darkness" on St. John's Eve. It is a protective and countermagic herb. The botanical name *hypericum* comes from the Greek and means "to protect" or "over an apparition." This refers to the belief that the plant could make evil spirits disappear. It was also called *Fuga Daemonum* ("flight of demons") because it repels evil spirits. It was believed to protect the wearer against all manner of evil.

Legend has it that the plant moves around to hide from those who seek its powers at Midsummer when it is made into garlands and charms to protect the home and livestock. It had to be gathered in a particular manner:

St. John's wort, St. John's wort,
I deem lucky the one who will have you;
I harvest you with my right hand,
I store you away with my left hand;
Whosoever finds you in the fold of young animals
Will never want for anything.[5]

Country folk often picked bunches of the herb and hung them in byres and stables to frighten evil spirits and keep the devil away. It was tossed onto the baal or hearth fires and allowed to burn to protect the home against lightning and storms. St. John's wort gathered at noon on Midsummer Day was reputed to be effective against several illnesses. It was also believed that the dew collected from the plant on Midsummer morning would preserve the eyes from disease, while the roots gathered at midnight on St. John's Eve would drive the devil and evil sorcerers away.

St. John's wort is ruled by the sun, the element of fire, and the sign of Leo. It is sacred to sun gods, particularly Baldur. It can be used in incenses to cleanse the working area, working tools, or the person. It repels negativity and can be used in purification and exorcism.

Old St. John's Wort Midsummer Love Charm

Legend has it that if a young woman should pick St. John's wort on the morning of Midsummer with the dew still fresh upon it, she will marry within a year.

St. John's Wort Yellow Dye

Used with alum the herb makes a yellow dye suitable for dyeing magical robes, cords, and altar cloths. Wash the fabric well, and while it is still wet begin the dyeing process. To make the dye, use two ounces of herb for every one ounce of fabric, plus one ounce of alum for every pound of fabric. Place the herb in a muslin bag, cover with a gallon of cold water, and slowly bring to a boil. Simmer until the fabric has acquired the color you desire.

Infused Oil

Loosely fill a glass jar with the leaves and flowers of St. John's wort and then fill to the top with a good vegetable oil, e.g., sunflower or almond oil. Cover the jar with a small piece of muslin and leave on a sunny windowsill for three to four weeks until the oil acquires a deep-red color. Strain the liquid through the muslin into a clean jar and seal. Externally the oil can be applied to bruises, wounds, varicose veins, ulcers, and sunburn.

N.B. With external use of St. John's wort, avoid prolonged exposure to sunlight.

St. John's Wort Tea

    2 tsps. St. John's wort flowers

    1 cup boiling water

Infuse for ten minutes and strain. The infusion is used for the treatment of anemia, rheumatism, headaches, nervous conditions, asthma, bronchial catarrh, irregular menstruation, mild depression, and insomnia. St. John's wort has been called "Nature's Prozac" and has been proven effective in the treatment of mild to moderate depression with fewer side effects than prescription antidepressants. As such, doctors in Continental Europe frequently prescribe it.

* N.B. The oil of St. John's wort should not be taken internally unless under qualified supervision. Both the oil and the infusion are phototropic and can cause skin irritation in direct sunlight. St. John's wort is not recommended for treating severe depression, and should not be taken with other prescription drugs.

Sunflower—Nothing visually evokes the warm summer sun as much as the giant yellow face of the sunflower, which moves during the day to follow the path of the sun across the sky. Magically it represents strength, courage, and action. The petals may be dried and used in incenses during sun rituals or during meditations and exercises designed to increase your confidence and self-image or to determine a course of positive action.

For the solstice feast, the seeds can be eaten raw or added to bread, cakes, and salads, or used as a coffee substitute. Romany Gypsies used to gather the buds just before they opened to use as a boiled vegetable.

N.B. Sunflower pollen and plant extracts may cause allergic reactions.

Sunflower Leaf Tea

> 1 young sunflower leaf, chopped
> 1 cup boiling water

Infuse for ten minutes and strain. Drink sweetened with a little honey if desired. Tea made from the leaves acts to reduce fevers. The Romanies and the Turks used it as a substitute for quinine.

Sunflower Charm to Attract Good Health

Thread a necklace of sunflower seeds and hang above your bed to attract good health.

Sunflower Happiness Bath

Sprinkle sunflower petals in your bath and soak up the sun power of the herb to increase your happiness.

Thyme *Thymus vulgaris*—Thyme is the name of a group of fragrant, shrubby, mint plants native to the Mediterranean region. The ancient Greeks used thyme as temple incense. Along with borage, thyme is an important herb for those following the warrior path seeking to refine their courage and their will. It may be used as incense to help focus personal energies and gain the strength to face difficulties ahead. It is also an herb of purification and protection and can be used to purify the working area.

N.B. Contact with fresh thyme may cause dermatitis and/or allergic reactions.

A Little Sprig of Thyme

Add thyme to food to bring back fun into the life of anyone who eats it. Throw a sprig into the Midsummer bonfire to attract good health, or wear a sprig in your hair to become irresistible!

A Fairy Herb

At midnight on Midsummer Eve, the King of the Fairies is said to dance with his followers on thyme beds. Thyme is one of the herbs that enables you to see fairies (see chapter 4 on Midsummer divination and magic).

Thyme Tea

2 tsps. dried thyme

1 cup boiling water

Infuse together for ten minutes. Strain and drink as a general tonic, to aid digestion, or to cure a hangover. It will also help alleviate nervousness and depression.

You can also use the infusion as a facial steam to cure acne and blemishes. Combine with rosemary in an infusion used as a final hair rinse to cure dandruff.

Vervain *Verbena officinalis*—Vervain is a hardy, herbaceous perennial native to Britain, Europe, North Africa and west Asia. Vervain is sacred to Cerridwen, a shapeshifter who has aspects as a cat goddess, a moon goddess, the harvest mother, and as a crone or white sow. Vervain is one of the sacred herbs of Midsummer. It will cleanse and purify as well as raise vibrations. It is sacred to poets and singers, heightens the consciousness, and intensifies clairvoyant powers. Use to invoke the deities Aphrodite, Aradia, Cerridwen, Diana, Galahad, Horus, Isis, Jupiter, Mars, Ra, Thor, Venus, and Zeus.

For magical purposes vervain should be gathered at the summer solstice. Gather enough for one year. Any vervain that has been leftover from last year's gathering should be cast onto the Midsummer bonfire.

Because of the Latin botanical name, many people confuse the druid herb vervain (Verbena officinalis) with lemon verbena (Aloysia triphylla), so make sure you've got the right one. I found at least one unscrupulous occult shop selling lemon verbena oil while calling it vervain oil.

Vervain Infusion

> 2 tsps. dried vervain
> 1 cup boiling water

Infuse for fifteen minutes, then strain and drink. This infusion may be used as a sedative. It strengthens the nervous system and relieves stress and tension. The tea can also be drunk before ritual to heighten the consciousness and enhance clairvoyant powers.

Druid's Vervain Lustral Water

> 5 tsps. dried vervain or 1 handful fresh vervain
> 2 cups boiling water

Infuse for ten minutes and then strain. Using fresh sprigs of vervain to sprinkle this water to ritually cleanse and purify a house or sacred space.

Violet (sweet) *Viola odorata*—Violet is a hardy perennial native to Europe and North Africa. The Greeks saw the violet as a symbol of fertility, sacred to Aphrodite, and frequently added it to love potions. Violets are a symbol of the constancy of love and fertility. Violets are associated with the twilight, a magical "time between times," when the Otherworld is nearer and is easier to slip into.

Sachet to Attract New Love

> Oblong of pink cloth
> 1 part violet flowers and leaves
> 1 part lavender flowers

Sew the herbs into the cloth and consecrate by holding in the smoke of some love incense (see the incense recipes at the end of this chapter). Place under your pillow for seven nights, and then hang in your bedroom window until your wish comes true.

Violet Tea

> 1 tsp. violet flowers and leaves
> ½ cup boiling water

Pour the water over the herb and infuse for five minutes. Strain and drink to ease sore throats, coughs, headaches, and insomnia.

Yarrow *Achillea millefolium*—Yarrow, native to the whole of Europe, is a hardy herbaceous perennial. It is sacred to the Horned God and to the male principle. Yarrow tea may be used when working on aspects of masculinity and for connection with the God. It may be used throughout the cycle of the wheel in incenses to invoke the God. Yarrow is one of the sacred herbs of Midsummer, assigned to St. John, and should be gathered for magical purposes or for extra healing power at the solstice. It can be used in incense or thrown onto the bonfire as an offering. Yarrow incense can be used to promote divination and clairvoyance.

To Ensure Love

On Midsummer morning cut nine heads of yarrow, saying:

> *I cut thee, yarrow, that love may grow.*

Take the yarrow home and bind the stems together with a green ribbon. Hang the charm above the bed that you share with your lover, and this will ensure lasting love.

Old Yarrow Love Charm

This rather gruesome verse was chanted over a piece of yarrow:

> *Green yarrow, green yarrow, you bear a white blow*
> *If my love loves me, my nose will bleed now.*
> *If my love don't love me, it 'ont bleed a drop*
> *If my love do love me, till bleed every drop.*

Yarrow Tea

> 2 tsps. yarrow
> 1 cup boiling water

Infuse for ten minutes, then strain and drink to ease fatigue, digestive problems, and to cleanse the entire body. This infusion can also be used for a facial steam and a tonic lotion. Add it to the bath to cleanse and invigorate.

*N.B. Large doses of yarrow may cause dermatitis. Yarrow should not be used by pregnant women.

Incense

Incenses, herbs, woods, and resins burned to release fragrant smoke have been used all over the world from ancient times to the present day. Rising smoke has always been associated with prayer rising to the gods, whether from the domestic hearth, the Pagan altar, the druid's needfire, or the Catholic Church's incense burner.

Incenses and oils work on several levels: The primary level is the effect it has on the mood of the magician. Any aromatherapist will tell you that perfumes affect the emotions. On a secondary level, a perfume may have certain associations for the person who experiences it. If you associate certain perfumes with a ritual setting, it can induce the mood required and concentrate your mind on the task at hand. If you condition yourself to associate different perfumes with different rituals or deities, this will act as a subconscious shortcut. On a tertiary and more profound level is the effect of the *vibration* of the perfume. When something vibrates at a given frequency, any object near it will begin to vibrate with the same frequency, a principle used in both healing and in magic. Each plant, like every crystal or stone, has a particular vibration. When we use an incense or oil, it is for the purpose of changing the vibration of the atmosphere to the level needed for a specific magical operation, not because it has a "nice smell."

There are several reasons why it is better to make your own incenses for magical purposes. Commercial incense sticks and cones are made with a compound base and synthetic, mineral-derived perfumes, and have no magical value. Make your own and you will be sure that they contain the correct ingredients and are blended in the proper manner at the right magically empowering time.

When it comes to blending incenses, plants can be used in many forms. Traditional Craft incenses are composed largely of flowers and herbs (leaves and stems), but incenses that contain resins, essential oils, and aesthetically pleasing shapes like star anise have become popular in recent years. Any herbs, flowers, berries, or barks used should be dried. For a real boost to the strength of an incense's perfume, add a few drops of essential oil.

Loose incense is probably the easiest type of incense to make, and the most useful kind for magical ritual. The recipes in this book are all for loose incense.

Making Incense

First of all assemble your ingredients, your pestle and mortar, your mixing spoons, and your jars and labels ready for the finished product.

All the measurements in this book are by volume, not weight, and I use a spoon to measure out small quantities when I am making a single jar of incense, and a cup for large quantities and big batches. Therefore, when the recipe says 3 parts frankincense, ½ part thyme, and 1 part myrrh, this means three spoonfuls of frankincense, half a spoonful of thyme, and one spoonful of myrrh.

When using resins and essential oils, these should be combined first, stirring  lightly with the pestle and left to go a little sticky before you add any woods, barks, and crushed berries. Next add any herbs and powders, and lastly any flowers.

Charging the Incense

As you blend the incense, concentrate on the purpose for which the incense will be used, and "project" this into the blend. If you like, you can make a whole ritual of the event, perhaps even picking and drying your own herbs, then laying out the tools and ingredients on the altar, lighting a candle, and asking the God and Goddess for help:

> *God and Goddess, deign to bless this incense, which I would consecrate in your names. Let it obtain the necessary virtues for acts of love and beauty in your honor. Let blessing be.*

The incenses should then be stored in screw-topped glass jars.

Burning Incenses

Loose incense is burned on individual, self-igniting charcoal blocks, or thrown directly onto the bonfire.

To use your incenses, take a self-igniting charcoal block (available from occult and church suppliers) and apply a match to it. It will begin to spark across its surface, and will eventually glow red. Place it on a flame-proof dish with a mat underneath (it will get very hot). When the charcoal block is glowing, sprinkle a pinch of the incense on top—a little goes a long way. Alternatively, if you are celebrating outdoors and have a bonfire, you can throw much larger quantities of incense directly onto the flames. I have also sprinkled it on the hot plate of my Rayburn (an old-fashioned, solid fuel stove), and this smolders away quite nicely, though it would really mess up a gas or electric hob!

Here is a useful tip: When a packet of charcoal blocks has been opened, the blocks will quickly start to absorb moisture from the air, which makes them difficult to ignite. Pop them in the oven for ten minutes at a low heat to dry them out, and they will light easily.

N.B. Contact with the following fresh herbs may cause dermatitis and/or allergic reactions:

Rue
Chamomile
Fennel
Sunflower
Thyme
Yarrow
Mugwort
Mandrake root
Horehound
Pennyroyal
Juniper berries
Peppermint (oil)

Solstice Sun Incense

½ part chamomile
½ part cinquefoil
1 part lavender flowers
½ part mugwort
1 part rose petals
½ part St. John's wort
½ part vervain
1 part orange peel
3 parts frankincense

Midsummer

3 parts red sandalwood
½ part mugwort
½ part chamomile flowers
½ part rose petals
½ part lavender flowers

Coamhain Incense

4 parts frankincense
2 parts red sandalwood
1 part heather flowers
½ part mint
½ part calendula
½ part fennel
½ part angelica
½ part St. John's wort
½ part chamomile

Amun Ra (Egyptian sun god)

½ part olive leaves
1 part cedar wood
1 pinch saffron
½ part reed stems
A few drops cedar oil
2 parts frankincense

Aphrodite (Greek goddess of love)

½ part cypress needles
A few drops cypress oil
3 parts benzoin
½ part rose petals
1 part apple wood
¼ part cinnamon sticks
¼ part daisy flowers
A few drops geranium oil
¼ part violet flowers

Apollo (Greek and Roman god of the sun, poetry, and medicine)

½ part bay laurel leaves
½ part peony flowers
2 parts aspen wood
2 parts frankincense
½ part cypress needles
½ part fennel seeds
2 parts acacia
A few drops bay oil

Arthur (Celtic sun god)

1 part apple blossoms
3 parts alder wood

Baldur (Scandinavian sun god)

1 part mistletoe
½ part St. John's wort flowers
2 parts oak bark
4 parts frankincense
½ part chamomile flowers

Bel (Sumerian sun god)

2 parts frankincense
½ part bistort root
A few drops frankincense oil
(optional)

Belinos (Celtic sun god)

2 parts willow bark
½ part daisy flowers
½ part celandine flowers
2 parts frankincense (optional)

Blodeuwedd (Welsh Flower Bride)

1 part broom flowers
1 part bean flowers
1 part horse chestnut flowers
(flowers only!)
1 part oak flowers
1 part meadowsweet flowers
1 part flowering nettle
1 part primrose flowers
1 part hawthorn flowers
1 part flowering burdock
1 part blackthorn flowers
1 part corn cockle flowers

Earth Mother

1 part pine resin
1 part mandrake root
1 part rose petals
½ part patchouli leaves
A few drops patchouli oil

Flora (Roman goddess of vegetation)

1 part hawthorn flowers
3 parts apple wood
½ part vine leaves
½ part rose petals
½ part cornflower petals

Gaia (Greek earth goddess)

1 part corn kernels
2 parts apple bark
½ part orange peel
A few drops orange oil
½ part vine leaves
½ part olive leaves
4 parts frankincense (optional)

Helios (Greek sun god)

½ part bay laurel leaves
½ part heliotrope (optional)
4 parts frankincense
A few drops cinnamon oil
½ part bistort root

Hera (Greek queen of heaven)

1 part apple blossom
2 parts willow
½ part iris petals
A few drops cypress oil
½ part red poppy petals
3 parts myrrh
1 part pear bark

Herakles/Hercules
(Greek deified sun hero)

2 parts apple bark
1 part cypress needles
2 parts oak bark
½ part aspen leaves
½ part olive leaves

Isis (Egyptian queen of heaven)

½ part heather
5 parts myrrh
½ part rose petals
¼ part vervain
¼ part wormwood
¼ part orris root powder
½ part ivy leaves
A few drops geranium oil
¼ part horehound
¼ part olive leaves
½ part white willow bark
2 parts cedar wood
A few drops cedar oil
½ part cypress needles
¼ part poppy seeds or petals
¼ part dragon's blood powder

Juno (Roman queen of heaven)

3 parts myrrh
A few drops myrrh oil
½ part olive leaves
½ part iris petals
½ part orris root powder

Mithras (Persian god of light/purity,
later god of sun/victory)

1 part cypress needles
A few drops cypress oil
2 parts myrrh
2 parts frankincense

Ra (Egyptian sun god)

1 part acacia
½ part mandrake
1 part chamomile flowers
A few drops chamomile oil
2 parts frankincense
2 parts myrrh
½ part bay leaves
½ part vine leaves
¼ part cinnamon powder
¼ part reed

Sun God

½ part fennel
½ part rue
½ part thyme
½ part chervil seed
½ part pennyroyal
1 part chamomile flowers
½ part geranium flowers
3 parts frankincense

Sun Goddess

3 parts frankincense
1 part cinnamon bark
A few drops ylang ylang oil
½ part lemon verbena

Fire Incense

2 parts oak wood
3 parts frankincense
1 part crushed juniper berries
A few drops orange oil
1 part sunflower petals
½ part rosemary
1 pinch saffron

Sun

2 parts acacia resin
3 parts frankincense
½ part orange peel
1 part myrrh
2 parts red sandalwood
½ part rosemary
¼ part cinnamon bark
1 part benzoin
A few drops cedar oil

Divination 1

½ part clove
1 part thyme
1 part lemon verbena
A few drops lemongrass oil

Divination 2

2 parts white sandalwood
1 part acacia
½ calendula (marigold) petals
1 part hazel wood
½ part bay
½ part clary sage
1 pinch nutmeg

Scrying

1 part mugwort
1 part valerian root
1 part anise
1 part wormwood
1 part St. John's wort
1 part dittany of Crete

Circle Invocation

3 parts frankincense
2 parts myrrh
1 part benzoin
½ part cinnamon
1 part rose petals
½ part vervain
½ part rosemary
2 parts sandalwood
¼ part bay

Healing

½ part bay leaves
½ part chamomile flowers
½ part lemon balm leaves
1 pinch powdered cinnamon
1 part crushed juniper berries
1 part lavender flowers
A few drops lavender oil
¼ part sage leaves
1 part rosemary leaves
A few drops rosemary oil

Reviving

1 part lemon balm leaves
1 part mint leaves
3 parts frankincense
A few drops lemon balm (melissa oil)
A few drops peppermint oil

Love

½ part thyme
3 parts red sandalwood
1 part red rose petals
A few drops bergamot oil
A few drops lavender oil
½ part lavender flowers
½ part basil

Protection

½ part bay
½ part avens
½ part mugwort
½ part yarrow
½ part rosemary
½ part St. John's wort
½ part angelica root
½ part basil
2 parts crushed juniper berries
A few drops juniper oil
3 parts frankincense
2 parts myrrh

Magical Oils

Magical oils have a number of uses. They can be used to consecrate magical tools, to anoint candles for magic, and to consecrate coveners as they enter the circle or sacred space. You might also wear a magical oil to evoke the power of a certain deity or season, or use it on an oil evaporator in place of incense in the circle. Here it represents the element of fire, unlike incense, which represents air.

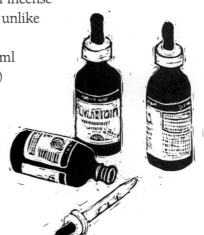

The following recipes are based on using 20 ml of base oil (sunflower, grapeseed, olive, almond) plus 20 drops of vitamin E oil to act as a preservative. Then add the recommended number of drops of essential oil—essential oils are always supplied in dropper bottles. Be sure to use 100 percent essential oils, not synthetic oils.

Amun Ra Oil

Frankincense 5, cinnamon 5, rose 8, myrrh 4

Apollo Oil

Cinnamon 9, myrrh 4, frankincense 2

Coamhain Oil

Chamomile 5, lavender 10, rose 10, verbena 10, orange 10, frankincense 3

Fire Oil

Orange 12, frankincense 4, sandalwood 4

Handfasting Oil

Rose 10, orange 4, cinnamon 2

Use to consecrate the rings that the couple will exchange during the ceremony.

Horus Oil

Marjoram 5, bergamot 10, sandalwood 10

Sun Goddess Oil

Cinnamon 6, lemon verbena 6, ylang ylang 6

---

1. John Stow, *Survey* (1598).

2. Sometimes this phrase refers to the real hand of an executed criminal, used in black magic. The fern hand is a truer Pagan tradition, and a lot less messy.

3. Traditional witches' chant.

4. E. Brewer, *Dictionary of Phrase and Fable* (London: Cassell and Co., 1885).

5. Alexander Carmichael, *Carmina Gadelica* (Edinburgh: Oliver and Boyd, 1928).

Traditional Midsummer Recipes

Food has always been an intrinsic part of seasonal celebrations. Food also plays a part in Craft ritual, and its production is one of the central themes of nature religions. Mysteriously, the small seed planted beneath the dark earth shoots and grows into something that will provide a sustaining meal. When it is placed it in the womb of Mother Earth, she nourishes and sustains it, magically transforming a tiny seed into a nourishing plant.

It is the custom to share food at the festivals and other ritual occasions of the Craft year. In the past, people were acutely aware of the passing of the seasons and of what each season had to offer in terms of food, herbs, and animal behavior. They were closely bound to the Wheel of the Year, its turning determining their activities—times for planting, times for weeding, times for gathering seeds, and times for harvest. During the summer and autumn a variety of plentiful food would be available, but during the winter there would only be stored produce and the few vegetable foods that survive the frosts. In a time when food is always available at the local store, we tend to forget the importance of the agricultural and pastoral year, which was everything to our ancestors. The festivals of the Craft attempt to make us more aware of the natural cycles and our part in them. In our seasonal celebrations, and in our feasts, we try to honor and reflect these magical connections of herbs and plants with the seasons.

The Ritual of the Cakes and Wine

For our ancestors one of the most valuable foods was grain, which could be made into flour and then bread, and it is one of the most important symbols of the nurturing Goddess. Bread is called "the staff of life" and sustains the body. Food is the basic necessity of existence, and bread came to symbolize ritually all other food.

When bread is consecrated it becomes the food of the spirit. Eating a thing is meant to impart something of its spirit to the consumer, and the ritual partaking of bread and wine constitutes absorbing the spirit of the God and Goddess. Eating bread and drinking wine was an important part of the rites of corn goddesses and vegetation gods.

While bread is often associated with the feminine, wine is associated with the masculine. Bread represents the earth and wine the heavens, bread the solid and wine the liquid, and the taking of the two together signifies the union of opposites. Wine was thought to feed not the body but the spirit with the divine inspiration of the God, freeing the imbiber from mundane thoughts and conventions, altering levels of consciousness and awakening the powers of the primal self within.

The dedication of the cakes and wine is one of the central points of any Craft ritual. It is the partaking of the sacrificed God of the corn and the body of the Goddess as Mother Earth, from whom all life stems. Christians believe that the bread and wine is the transubstantiated flesh and blood of God. Looking at it this way, we can understand that the cakes and wine are magically changed during the ritual of consecration, and partake of the power of the gods.

The cup is the equivalent of the cauldron or grail, which contained wisdom and inspiration. During the consecration the priest and priestess may perform the act together, or one or the other may bless them.

The Ceremony of the Cakes and Wine

When the work of the ritual is accomplished, the cakes and wine are blessed and shared. Take the wine and pour it into the cup, saying:

Lord and Lady, I call upon you to bless this wine, the blood of the earth pressed smooth. As we drink of thee, may we learn of the wisdom of the Goddess.

The wine is passed around clockwise. Take the cakes, saying:

Lord and Lady, I call upon thee to bless these cakes, the fruit of the womb of the Goddess, without which we would not live. As we eat of thee, may we learn of the love of the Goddess.

The cakes are passed around.

Seasonal Recipes

By this time of year food is plentiful with salad vegetables, soft fruits, and herbs in peak condition. The quantities of ingredients for these recipes are listed in three types of measurement:

American (U.S.) Imperial Metric

In some cases they have been rounded up or down, so make sure you stick with one set of measurements for each recipe.

Coamhain Soup

	American (U.S.)	Imperial	Metric
Cucumber	½	½	½
Tomatoes	7 cups	2 lbs.	900 g
Green bell pepper	1	1	1
Onion	1	1	1
Garlic cloves	2	2	2
Bread slices	2	2	2
Olive oil	2–3 tbsp.	2–3 tbsp.	25–40 ml
Water	5 cups	2 pints	1 liter

Chili powder	½ tsp.	½ tsp.	2 g
Black pepper	Pinch	Pinch	Pinch

Blanch and skin the tomatoes. Put everything into a blender and blend. Heat through.

Comfrey Fritters

Egg white	1	1	1
Cornstarch/cornflour	½ cup	2 oz.	50 g
Water	2 tbsps.	2 tbsps.	25 ml
Young comfrey leaves			

Beat the egg white until it forms stiff peaks. Blend the cornstarch with the water until it forms a smooth cream and fold it into the egg white. Dip the leaves in this batter and deep-fry until golden.

Comfrey is an herb of protection and healing, and is particularly potent at Midsummer.

Elderflower Fritters

Heads of elderflowers	6	6	6
Egg whites	2	2	2
Cornstarch/cornflour	1 cup	4 oz.	100 g
Water			
Sugar to sweeten			

Mix the cornstarch with enough cold water to form a thin paste. In a separate bowl, whisk the egg whites until fairly stiff. Add a little sugar and continue to whisk for another minute. Carefully fold the egg whites into the cornstarch paste to make a light, frothy batter. Dip the elderflower heads into this batter and deep-fry them until golden brown. While still hot, roll the fritters in sugar and serve immediately.

Gooseberry Fool

Gooseberries	3½ cups	14 oz.	400 g
Butter	4 tbsps.	2 oz.	50 g
Sugar to sweeten			
Light/single cream	1¼ cups	½ pint	285 ml
Egg yolks	3	3	3

Wash the gooseberries and stem them. Put them in a pan with the butter and gently heat. Cook on a low heat until soft. Crush the gooseberries with a wooden spoon and sweeten with sugar to taste. In another pan bring the cream to a boil. Remove the pan from the heat and whisk in the egg yolks. Set the pan over a larger one of hot water and stir briskly until the mixture thickens. Cool. Add the gooseberries. Spoon into individual serving glasses and chill to set.

In the south of England, Midsummer Day is the time when gooseberries are officially ripe.

Elderflower Champagne

Elderflower heads	5 pints	4 pints	2 liters
Cold water	5 qts.	1 gallon	4.5 liters
Lemon	1	1	1
Sugar	3¼ cups	1½ lbs.	680 g
White wine vinegar	2 tbsps.	2 tbsps.	25 ml
Campden tablets	2	2	2

Dissolve the sugar in warm water and allow it to cool. Squeeze the juice from the lemon and chop the lemon rind roughly. Place the elderflowers in a bowl and add the vinegar. Pour on the rest of the water and add the campden tablets. Steep for four days. Strain the infusion well so that all solid matter is excluded, and bottle in screw-top bottles. The elderflower champagne will be ready to drink in seven days. This is a very hit-and-miss recipe—sometimes it works and sometimes it doesn't. If there is no sign of the natural yeast present in the flowers working after a day or two, try adding a little activated yeast.

The elder blossom at Midsummer represents the Goddess, and this is the traditional time to gather the flowers for wine and the leaves for healing salves.

Anise Tea

    1 tsp. (4 g) seeds
    1 cup boiling water

Infuse, covered, for fifteen minutes. Strain and serve, adding a little sugar or honey to taste.

Anise is sacred to the Sun God.

Clary Sage Tea

    2 tsps. (8 g) dried herb
    1 cup boiling water

Infuse for fifteen minutes and strain, adding a little sugar or honey to taste.

Clary sage is an herb of divination. It is traditionally used at Midsummer, when the entrance to the Otherworld is sometimes visible in the owl light of dusk and dawn.

Mint Tea

    2 tsps. (8 g) dried herb
    1 cup boiling water

Infuse the mint in the boiling water for ten minutes. Strain and serve, adding a little sugar or honey to taste.

Mint tea is very useful as a restorative during the long watch of Midsummer Eve from dusk until dawn.

Strawberry Wine

Strawberries	5 qts.	1 gallon	4.5 liters
Sugar	8 cups	3½ lbs.	1.5 kg
Raisins	1¾ cups	½ lb.	225 g
Water	5 qts.	1 gallon	4.5 liters
Yeast, dried	1 package	1 package	1 package

Mash the strawberries and add the water. Let stand for 24 hours, strain off the liquor, and add the sugar and raisins. Return to the brewing bin. Stir in the sugar until it has dissolved, and add the yeast. Cover and stand for two days, stirring daily. Transfer to a demijohn and fit an airlock. This wine should be ready to bottle in six months.

Strawberry wine is drunk at Midsummer to facilitate contact with the fairy Wildfolk. Strawberries are sacred to the Mother Goddess who nurtures all living things.

Black Mead

Black currants	7 pints	4 lbs.	2 kg
Honey	4 cups	2 lbs.	1 liter
Red grape concentrate	1¼ cups	½ pint	285 ml
Malic acid	1½ tsps.	¼ oz.	7 g
Water	5 qts.	1 gallon	4.5 liters
Yeast and nutrient			

Mash the black currants and put them in a brewing bin. Boil the water and add the honey to it, stirring to dissolve. Pour this over the black currants and cool to room temperature (20° C). Add the yeast and nutrient according to the manufacturer's instructions, and let stand for three days in a warm place, stirring daily. Add the concentrate and malic acid. Strain into a demijohn and fit an airlock.

Sack

Fennel roots	3	3	3
Sprays rue	2	2	2
Honey	8 cups	4 lbs.	2 liters
Juice of 2 lemons			
Yeast and nutrient			
Water	5 qts.	1 gallon	4.5 liters

Wash the fennel roots and boil them in water for forty minutes. Strain and return to the pan. Add the honey and boil for two hours. Skim off any scum. Cool to room temperature (20° C) and add the lemon juice. Then add the yeast and nutrient according to the manufacturer's instructions. Strain into demijohns and fit an airlock. This dry sack will be ready for drinking after a year.

This is a traditional English mead drink mentioned by Shakespeare and others.

*N.B. Contact with fresh fennel or rue may cause dermatitis and/or allergic reactions.

Heather Ale

Heather shoots	5 cups	2 pints	1.1 liters (600 g)
Sugar	2¼ cups	1 lb.	450 g
Yeast, dried	1 pack	1 pack	1 pack
Malt	2 cups	1 lb.	450 g
Water	9½ qts.	2 gallons	9 liters

Put the heather in a pan, cover with water, and boil for fifteen minutes. Strain into a brewing bin and add the sugar and malt. Stir to dissolve. Add the rest of the water and cool to room temperature (20° C). Add the activated yeast and cover. Let stand for five days and pour into screw-top bottles. It will be ready to drink after seven days.

The Picts brewed a legendary ale from heather, the recipe for which was a secret. Invading Norsemen tortured the guardians of the secret in order to obtain the recipe, but to no avail. Heather is a sacred plant of Midsummer and represents the spirit of the vegetation god.

Midsummer Rituals

This chapter contains the text for several rituals in a variety of traditions. But first, here are some basic instructions for creating a sacred space, casting a circle, and dissolving the circle in indoor and outdoor rituals.

Basic Instructions for Indoor Rituals

Creating a Sacred Space for Indoor Rituals

The room in which you are to work should be cleared of as much furniture as is physically possible. The room should be thoroughly cleaned. Purify the room with cleansing incense such as frankincense or rosemary, or lustral water if you have it.

The Altar

A low table or chest can be used as an altar. This should be placed in the north (you might need a compass to find the cardinal points). Cover it with a white cloth. On it place something to represent the Goddess and the God—what this might be is up to you. Some people have statues, but if you don't, think carefully about something natural that represents the deities to you. I have a pair of stag horns to represent the God, but it could be a pine cone or a stone. Use your imagination and what seems right to *you*. The Goddess image is placed on the left, and the God image on the right.

Place three candles in holders on the altar. I use white, red, and black ones to represent the three stages of the Goddess, but you might like to use colors suitable to the occasion.

A dish of salt and a dish of water are placed near the front. A plate of bread or cakes and some wine in an open bottle or jug are placed to one side. You will need a cup or goblet for drinking the wine, and some people insist on a pentacle of clay or copper being placed on the altar. You will also need a knife that you keep for ritual purposes, which some people call an *athame*. In the old days the cup was simply the best cup in the house, and the knife one kept aside. These days people buy or make special equipment, which is nice but not necessary.

You can also decorate the altar with seasonal flowers. Place a dish of incense on it, too.

The Quarters

A candle is placed in each of the quarters. The colors chosen help resonate with the vibration of that quarter: green for the north (earth), yellow for the east (air), red for the south (fire), and blue for the west (water). If you can't get these you can use white candles, but the more you can reinforce the imagery the more it helps your visualization. Some people also like to place objects that represents the elements in the quarters—perhaps a dish of earth in the north, the incense in the east, a flame or candle in the south, and a dish of water in the west.

Check that you have everything you need within the circle (remember the matches!) before you start, as once the circle is cast, you will not be able to leave to get anything.

Casting a Circle for Indoor Rituals

Light the incense. The first act that must be performed is to establish the boundaries of the circle. Take the knife, and beginning in the north draw the circle around the room. Remember that where the point of the knife draws will be the edge of the circle. Include in the circle all the things and people you wish to be within the circle for the rite. Take the knife and place the tip in the bowl of salt, saying:

> Be this salt dedicated to the Lord and Lady to keep us from evil and protect us in this time.

Take the knife again and place the tip in the bowl of water, saying:

> Be this water dedicated to the Lord and Lady to keep us from peril and to purify this place.

Tip the water into the salt and mix them together. Sprinkle clockwise (deosil) around the circle, saying:

> May we cast from us all evil and darkness, viciousness, and malice. May we become that which we must be before the Lord and Lady, seeking ill to no one. May we be clean within and without so that we are acceptable before them.

Finish by sprinkling each person in turn.

Next connect the circle to all three realms by invoking the axis mundi. Take the knife and stand in the center of the circle. Point it above and say:

> Powers of the worlds above, I do summon, stir, and call you up to guard our circle and to witness our rites.

Bring the knife down in a straight line and point it downward. Say:

> Powers of the worlds below, I do summon, stir, and call you up to guard our circle and to witness our rites.

The circle is then invoked. Take the knife and begin in the north and move around to the east. The casting of the circle is always begun in the north, as this is the root of power that flows from north to south, so the power gateway is opened.[1] Draw a pentacle in the east and say:

O mighty powers of the east, I do summon, stir, and call you up to guard our circle and to witness our rites.

Repeat this in the south, west, and north.

Return to the altar and consecrate the altar candles with these words:

Be to me the fire of moon,
Be to me the fire of night,
Be to me the fire of joy,
Turning darkness into light,
By the Virgin, waxing cold,
By the Mother, full and bold,
By the Hag Queen, silent, old,
By the moon, the one in three,
Consecrated, blessed be.

Light the candles and take one around to light all the quarter candles. If you wish, you can carry the dish of incense around the circle.

The God and the Goddess are then invoked:[2]

(Goddess name),[3] *I invoke and call upon thee, threefold Goddess of the moon,* (Goddess name), *queen of the moonlit sea, fairer than night and silver clad, thee I invoke. Mother of the moon and calm waters, let thy light fall upon us for thy hair is a pool of stars in the darkness. I call upon thee, widow of the waning moon whose children have left thee to sorrow. Guard us with learning and grant us a place in thy dark cloak of understanding. Thee I invoke. Descend, I beseech thee, and be with us now.*

The God is then invoked:

(God name),[4] *Lord of the heaven and power of the sun. Lord of the hunt and forests. I invoke thee in thy secret name of* (God name). *Come unto us and honor our circle, we beg of you. Mighty one, our Lord, all honor to thee, consort of the Goddess. Come, I call upon thee. Descend, I beseech thee, and be with us now.*

The purpose of the ritual is then stated:

Lord and Lady, God and Goddess, sacred pair that were with us before the dawn of time and shall be until its dusk, hear now the purpose of this ritual and witness it. (State the purpose).[5]

The circle dance is performed to raise power. Everyone links hands and circles the fire or cauldron placed in the center of the circle, chanting:

Thrice about the altar go
Once for Virgin pure as snow,
Once for Full Moon's soft sweet breath,
Once for Dark Moon, old as death,
Thrice about the altar spin
That the rite shall well begin.

The work of the ritual is now performed.

Dissolving the Circle in Indoor Rituals

When all is finished, the circle is dissolved. Take the knife and cut through the boundary of the circle near the east and say:

Mighty powers of the east, thank you for guarding our circle and for witnessing our rites. I bless you in the name of the Lord and the Lady.

Repeat in all the other three directions. Cut through the center and thank the powers of above and below. The Lord and Lady are not dismissed but thanked:

Companions, we have met together this night to celebrate the feast of (or whatever the purpose was). *Together we have worked for our purposes. The God and Goddess have witnessed our workings and only they will measure purposes and our hearts. Together we have invoked for power to accomplish our working, but it is not for us to command those whom we worship. Nor is it for us to bid them be gone. We cannot dismiss them. I ask instead of the Lord and Lady,* (God and Goddess names), *that they are with us all our days, guiding our feet and lighting our paths. I ask that the Lord and Lady are with us in our lives and in our deaths, our true parents, even as we are their children. Let the circle be extinguished but let us not forget the workings of this night. Let the candles be put out but let us not forget what we have learned. Let the rite be ended now in the knowledge we shall meet once more.*

Before the Lord and Lady, (God and Goddess names), *God and Goddess, the rite is ended. Blessed be.*

Put out the candles and dismantle the temple.

Basic Instructions for Outdoor Rituals

When working indoors it is usual to incorporate a greater degree of ritual in order to build the atmosphere. Outdoors it is much easier to feel the connections with the web, and usually the rituals are much simpler and often more powerful.

The altar may be a simple cloth on a tree stump or rock, or on the ground. Candles in jars can be placed on the altar and at the quarter points. The candles are lit and the axis mundi is invoked (see the instructions for invoking the axis mundi in the section "Casting a Circle for Indoor Rituals" in this chapter). The circle is drawn with the knife, pausing to invoke the quarters at the cardinal points. The Lord and Lady are invoked and the purpose of the ritual stated. A circle dance to the accompaniment of music or chanting is performed around the fire or cauldron in the center. The working of the night is then done. The cakes and wine are blessed and shared, and the circle is dismantled in the order it was created.

Everything should be collected and taken home with you. Do not leave candle stubs or incense behind. Do not leave crystals. The only thing I leave is some cake for the forest spirits, and I always pour a libation of wine on the ground.

Rite for Midsummer

The altar should be decorated with golds and yellows—this theme is echoed through the candles, cloths, and flowers, which might include the traditional summer herbs of St. John's wort, fennel, marigold, chamomile, chervil, and marjoram. A sun wheel or sun representation should be centrally placed. The bonfire, if you have one, should contain oak wood. If not, a yellow or gold candle can be placed in the center of the circle. The cauldron is filled with water and flowers.

Cast the circle as described in the instructions for indoor or outdoor rituals, depending on where you are holding your celebration.

Priestess: (faces south, the direction of Midsummer and the element of fire)

Lord of heaven and power of the sun, we invoke thee in thy secret name of (God name),[6] O Lord of the greatest light. Now is the time of thy glory and power. Place your shield between us and all power of darkness. Shoot forth your arrows of light to protect us. Grant to us at this time green fields and good hunting. Give to us orchards of fullness and corn that has risen high. Show us within thy time of splendor the pathway to the peace of the Lord and Lady.

She draws a pentacle above the altar and then plunges the tip of her wand into the cauldron:[7]

The knife to the cup, the rod to the cauldron, the sun to the earth, but the flesh to the spirit.

The priest turns to the priestess and salutes her. He speaks the words of ancient wisdom.

Priest:

Now is the time of the sun in its glory when our Lord, (God name),[8] is at his height in the heavens. Yet it must also be remembered that now is also the time of (God name[9])'s decline to his death and rebirth at the darkest time of winter. As it is with the God, so it is with man. We also journey throughout our time, from birth until death and to rebirth on our way. We must remember that the Goddess will raise the God with the kiss of rebirth and send him, yet again, on his journey. We also go down to the cloak of (Goddess name[10])'s darkness and her veil hides us from mortal sight. But the tomb is the womb of time from which we return to other lives, to share once more the knowledge and love of our fellows and friends.

Priestess:

> *Dance, one and all, dance about the cauldron of our Craft. Be blessed by the waters of (Goddess name)[11] that are contained in the cauldron, and remember that which you have heard this night.*

The coven members dance three times around the cauldron, and the priestess sprinkles them with water. This is the time when fire jumping takes place.

Everyone sits down around the fire, and the vigil begins to await the dawn. Now is the time to share the wine and engage in divination, feasting, and casting incense in the fire.

When the dawn breaks, dissolve the circle. Taking a light from the fire, go to wherever you can to watch the sun come up, which is encouraged with chanting and drumming and traditionally the firing of flaming reed arrows into the sky. Firebrands are then taken around the fields to encourage the crops.[12]

When the fire has gone out, take some of the ashes to be scattered in the fields and gardens to encourage their fertility.

The Rite of the Oak King and the Holly King

The altar should be decorated with golds and the traditional summer herbs of St. John's wort, fennel, marigold, chamomile, chervil, and marjoram. The bonfire, if you have one, should contain oak wood. If not, a yellow or gold candle can be placed in the center of the circle in the cauldron.

This ritual is for a minimum or four celebrants, two of which take on the role of Oak King and Holly King. Women can take on these roles if there are not enough men present. They should prepare wreaths of oak and holly, respectively. The other celebrants can wear chaplets of the sacred Coamhain herbs and flowers.

Cast the circle.

Priestess:

The Goddess is in her glory, walking among us clad in white, red, and golden yellow. Where she steps grow fruits and blooming flowers. Around her lovely body, from hip to shoulder, she swings a mantle, lustrous black, embroidered with the stars of the heavens and the silvered moon. This is our Goddess, our wondrous queen.

Priest:

Now is the time of the summer solstice, the time of greatest light. We gather here to celebrate the time of brightness. Now is the time of the sun when our Lord is at his height in the heavens. Yet it must also be remembered that now is also the time of his decline to his death and rebirth at the darkest time of winter.

Priestess:

The strength of the old king is waning and a new suitor stands ready to challenge for the hand of the Goddess.

Priest:

The king of the waxing year and the king of the waning year must do battle on this day.

Priestess:

The lord of the waxing year is represented by the Oak King, the ruler of this day.

Priest:

Come forward, the Oak King.

The man playing the Oak King steps forward.

Priestess:

Yet on this day his brother, lord of the waning year, stands ready to take the land into his keeping. He is represented by the Holly King.

Priest:

Come forward, the Holly King.

The man playing the Holly King steps forward.

Priest:

    Now is the time when the forces of light and darkness do battle.

Priestess: (crowning the Oak King with his oak wreath)

    I crown you the Oak King, lord of the waxing year. Now is the time of your greatest power. Are you ready to do battle for the hand of our Goddess?

Oak King:

    I am.

Priestess: (crowning the Holly King with his wreath)

    I crown you the Holly King, lord of the waning year. Your season is almost upon us. Are you ready to do battle for the hand of our Goddess?

Holly King:

    I am.

There follows a choreographed battle between the Holly King and Oak King, at the end of which the Oak King falls to the floor. If there is not sufficient room for such a battle to take place, a symbolic passing of a scepter or similar object can be substituted.

Priestess:

    Holly King, lord of the waning year, I name you the victor. Now is the time you take up the scepter and rule the land of the Goddess until the time of the winter solstice, when once again you will do battle with your brother.

Holly King:

    As it is with the God, so it is with man. We also journey throughout our time, from birth until death and to rebirth on our way. We must remember that the Goddess will raise the God with the kiss of rebirth and send him, yet again, on his journey. We also go down to the cloak of her darkness and her veil hides us from mortal sight. But the tomb is the womb of time from which we return to other lives, to share once more the knowledge and love of our fellows and friends.

The cakes and wine are shared. The rite may be completed with divination, story-telling, and spell casting. The circle is then dissolved.

Witch Rite for Midsummer Day

The place of meeting is decorated with oak boughs, leaves, and acorns. Before the rite music, dancing and games take place to evoke the high-spirited feeling of summer. Couples perform whirling dances, and a large sun wheel is rolled about in sport. This wheel is later placed to the side of the altar during the rite. A *labrys* (a Cretan, two-headed moon ax) or fabricated, two-headed ax is also placed by the altar or hung upright behind it. The altar is placed in the north of the circle and also acts as a throne for the priestess, who embodies the Goddess during the ritual. Short robes rather than long, cumbersome ones are worn, as this rite involves a lot of movement and dancing.

This rite includes an old folk song, itself perhaps a fragment of old, shape-changing lore. According to the legends of the Craft, shape-changing can occur during this rite.

A fifteen-foot circle is cast.

Priestess: (standing in the north with the altar behind her)

Witches all, in ages far past it was the custom on this day for the king and lord to be sacrificed in a magical ceremony, that famine, storm, and war should not afflict the people, that crops should grow tall and golden. Darkness was removed from many souls by the courage of the man who walked willingly and courageously to his doom. The funeral rites were deeply emotional and made a strong impression, but far greater was the magical portion of the rite, unseen and unseeable by human eyes, stronger and far more ancient. Such magic as this was cruel and powerful but it worked magnificently.

She sits on the altar, as on a throne. The priest stands in her place, with arms held out in invocation.

Priest:

On this night we gather here to perform again, in symbol and magical dance, the rite of the Oak King's sacrifice as it was done in ages past. In this day the Lady no longer requires the sacrifice of any among us, and the night that falls is sweet.

He turns to the priestess and salutes her with his athame, saying:

O laughing, naked queen, beautiful and yet terrible. Thou, who like all women, canst make then destroy thy men, yet art beyond all blame; for thou art the Goddess. Be with us here. As thy holy labrys has two edges, so thou hast two faces. One serene, lovely, and clear as the silver moon, the other dark, awesome, and cruel, for thou art as all women.

He salutes her with his athame.

The priestess sits at the south of the altar, her arms held out like the crescent of the moon.

Priest:

Thou who above all art adored, know that thy worshippers do give thee obeisance. The wise, the strong, and the powerful, and the very princes of the world do honor unto thee. . . .

He hands her the coven sword, which she holds before her like a scepter. He kneels and says:

The Goddess is kind when it pleases her. Thou who art the day art also the night, and the time now doth require night, darkness, and strife among men for thy purposes.

The priest stands back with the men near the edge of the circle. The priestess stands puts down the sword, and commands music. She leads the women around the edge of the circle five times deosil in a stately dance. Then she leads them five times around the edge of the circle widdershins in a wild, whirling dance, accompanied by whoops and cries. Each woman then returns to her male partner at the edge of the circle.

The priestess returns to her place on the altar.

Priestess:

The life is of the wheel is thirteen moons with all the seasons around; the life of the king shall likewise pass from birth unto the ground.

She signals for music to begin again, and the men dance sunwise around the circle following the priest who chants the following, one line at a time, with the men repeating each line, imitating the creatures mentioned with one perambulation around the circle for each line:

I am a stag of seven tines for strength
I am a flood across a plane for extent
I am a wind on a deep lake for depth
I am a ray of the sun, opulent
I am a hawk above the cliffs, for cunning
I am a bloom among flowers for excellence
I am a wizard
Who but I brings forth the hilltop's magic fire
I am a spear with lust for life in vengeance
I am a salmon in a pool of swiftness
I am a hill where poets walk for wisdom
I am a boar strong and red for power and valor
I am a breaker threatening doom for terror
I am a sea tide that drags to death for night.

All sit as the priest invokes the final line:

Who but I knows the secret of the unhewn dolmen.

He throws incense into the brazier and sits. All may drink wine and rest at this time.

The priestess stands with arms outstretched and says:

When the call comes the man does not willingly come until the libation has been made with love and with pain. Under the chase there is a transformation that can stir our powers.

She signals for music to begin again. The women form a circle in the center, facing outward, while the men form a ring facing inward. As the men chant they dance, while the women stay silent and watch. While the women chant and dance, the men stay silent and watch. As the lines are chanted the participants imitate the animals mentioned, trying to feel the animal deep within them.

Men and women:

Cunning and art we do not lack
But I with a whistle will fetch him back

Men:

> O I shall go into a hare
> With sorrow and sighing and mickle care
> And I shall go in the Horned God's name,
> Aye, until I be fetched hame!

Women:

> Hare take heed
> Of a bitch Greyhound
> Who'll harry thee
> All these fields around
> For here I come in the Lady's name
> All but for to fetch thee hame!

Men and women:

> Cunning and art we do not lack
> But I with a whistle will fetch him back

Priest:

> Yet I shall go into a trout
> With sorrow and sighing and mickle doubt
> And show thee many a crooked game
> Ere I be fetchéd hame!

Women:

> Trout take heed of an otter lank
> Who'll harry thee close
> From bank to bank
> For here come I in the Lady's name
> All but for to fetch thee hame!

Men and women:

> Cunning and art we do not lack
> But I with a whistle will fetch him back

Priest:

> But I shall go into a bee
> With mickle horror
> And dread of thee
> And flit to hive in the Horned God's name
> Ere that I be fetchéd hame!

Women:

> Bee take heed of a red, red, hen
> She'll harry thee close
> Through door and pen
> For here I come in the Lady's name
> All but for to fetch thee hame!

Men and women:

> Cunning and art we do not lack
> But I with a whistle will fetch him back

Men:

> Yet I shall go into a mouse
> And haste me into the Miller's house;
> There in his corn
> To have good game
> Ere that I be fetched hame!

Women:

> Mouse take heed of the white tib cat
> That never was baulked by mouse or rat
> For I'll crack thy bones in our Lady's name
> Thus shalt thou be fetched hame!

Men and women:

> Cunning and art we do not lack
> But I with a whistle will fetch him back!

At the conclusion, all drop.

Priest:

> As one generation doth pass and the next comes thereafter, so have thy secret people always continued. Thou hast returned to us, O Lady. Return we ask to the world outside and bring back again the ancient ecstasy of joy and terror and beauty most sublime.

Priestess:

> Eko, Eko, Azarak
> Eko, Eko, Zomelak
> Eko, Eko, Cernunnos
> Eko, Eko, Aradia

She salutes the altar with her athame. The priest dissolves the circle and declares:

> The rite is ended. Until we gather once again, merry meet and merry part, and merry meet again.

Cornish Flower Ritual

This ritual is a public rite, ostensibly performed by non-Pagans in Cornwall at Midsummer. It follows the theme of the flower bride. The ceremony itself is spoken in Cornish and it climaxes with the Lady of the Flowers casting into the bonfire a bunch of herbs, both good herbs and bad weeds.

Ordenary:

> Herwyth usadow agan
> hendasow yn termynyow kens,
> Awotta ny ow cul agan Tansys Golowan,
> haneth yn cres an Haf.
> Tan y'n cunys
> Lemmyn gor uskys,
> May tewo an Tansys
> Yn Hanow Dew!

Arlodhes an Blejyow:

> Otta kelmys yn-kemyskys
> Blejyow, may fons-y cowl leskys,

Ha'n da, ha'n drok.
Re dartho an da myl egyn,
Glan re bo dyswres pup dregyn,
Yn tan, yn mok!

Ordenary:

Towl lemmyn an blejyow!

Translation:

Master of Ceremonies:

According to the custom of our
forefathers in days of old,
Behold us making our Midsummer Bonfire,
This night in the middle of Summer
Now set the pyre
At once on fire,
Let flame aspire
In God's high Name!

Lady of the Flowers:

In one bunch together bound
Flowers for burning here are found
Both good and ill.
Thousandfold let good seed spring
Wicked weeds, fast withering,
Let this fire kill!

Master of Ceremonies:

Now cast the flowers!

The flowers are cast into the bonfire.

Summer Lustration Ritual

This ritual is performed at the rising of the sun on the day of the summer solstice. It may form the conclusion of a night-long vigil from the eve before. The circle is cast as the dawn is breaking by the priestess (if it has not already been cast as part of a previous Midsummer Eve rite).

Priest:

This is the time of greatest light, and we embrace the light within ourselves.

Priestess:

The earth is in full greening. The flowers blossom. Mother Earth is in full bearing.

He takes a glass vessel of water and the group waits in silent meditation for the sun to rise and illuminate the vessel and charge the water.

Priest:

Lord of the sun, we call upon thee. Consort of the Goddess, I call upon thee. Lord of the Green, I call upon thee. Charge this vessel with thy power.

Priestess: (taking the vessel from him)

As we drink, let us embrace the light within us.

She drinks and the vessel is passed around so that all may drink and each repeats her words. The priest drinks last.

Priest:

Let the light grow within us.

The remaining water is sprinkled with a sprig of vervain or rosemary over each person present as an act of ritual cleansing.

The circle is closed. If it is not possible to perform this ceremony, you can put out a glass vessel of water to be charged by the rising sun, and drink it as you awake.

Drawing Down the Sun

If you have read any books on Wicca you will have heard the phrase "drawing down the moon," during which a priestess calls down the power of the moon. But you may not have heard the phrase "drawing down the sun," equally important in traditional witchcraft. This is performed at each of the festivals celebrated with fire, including, of course, the summer solstice. While the moon's image is captured in a boat of glass, the rays of the sun are concentrated on a lens and projected onto tinder, thus causing a flame to be lit directly from the divine sun. This type of fire is called *need fire*, *wildfire*, or *elf fire* and is a protection against evil and a means of purification. Fires caused by lightning or by the friction of two pieces of wood from a tree dedicated to the sky god (like oak) has the same value. They have a celestial and therefore magically potent origin.[13]

One traditional method was practiced in Wales in the Vale of Glamorgan. Nine men would remove all metals from their persons and go into the nearest woods to collect wood from nine different trees. A circle was cut in the ground and the wood laid crosswise over it, and then two pieces of oak were rubbed together until a spark set the fire going. The oak (*duir* = "door") flowers at Midsummer and marks the door opening on one side to the waxing year and on the other side to the waning year. Midsummer fires always contain oak.

Litha: A Saxon Midsummer Celebration

As everyone gathers for the festival, they are greeted by the Mead Bearer with goblets of mead.

The altar is set up in the north and covered with a cloth.

The ceremony begins with a hammer-hallowing equivalent of the Wiccan circle casting with an athame. The circle is invoked with Thor's Hammer (a symbol in the shape of an inverted *T*), consecrating the place of ritual. First the circle is drawn on the ground with the hammer, and must be big enough to contain all the celebrants. It is usual to start in the east and

work clockwise around the circle. A branch dipped in water is then used to sprinkle and purify the circle.

The quarters are then invoked with the hammer by the *gothi* (priest). Beginning at the east the cardinal points are invoked:

EAST: I invoke Austri, guardian of the east. Welcome Odin and Frigga. Welcome spirits of the winds.

SOUTH: I invoke Sudri, guardian of the south. Welcome Thor and Sif, Baldur and Nanna. Welcome spirits of fire.

WEST: I invoke Westri, guardian of the west. Welcome Heimdall. Welcome spirits of the rivers and sea.

NORTH: I invoke Nordri, guardian of the north. Welcome Frey and Freya. Welcome Erce. Welcome spirits of earth.

Priest: (goes to the center of the circle and place the hammer there)
I create here a link to Yygdrasil and the nine worlds. Welcome here all gods. Welcome here all spirits. Welcome here all men and women. Let no one disturb this sacred place hallowed with Thor's sign and now under the protection of the Thunderer.

Priestess:
I welcome the spirits of this land here on Midsummer Day to celebrate the time of Baldur's brightness.

She pours an offering of mead on the ground for the local spirits of the land.
Now is the time of greatest light, when winter and hunger are banished. The land is green and fertile. The harvest time approaches, the bounty of the sun and earth, fruit of their sacred marriage. The corn, which we call in poetic fashion "Sif's golden hair," will ripen in the light of the sun.

The drinking horn is filled with mead and passed around the circle with this blessing:

Mead Bearer:
Let all drink, and as they drink add their blessings.

All drink and as they do they add an extempore blessing.

Priest:

> We, too, shall harvest the rewards of our actions, be they good or ill. Now is the time to reflect on our works, our thoughts, and our plans as the year turns from wax-ing to waning.

The drinking horn is filled and passed again. As each person drinks, they may say something in praise of the season.

Priest:

> Thor the Thunderer, give us your protection.

Priestess:

> Sif the golden haired, grant blessing on the ripening grain.

Priest:

> Frey, grant blessing on the beasts of the field.

Priestess:

> Freya, grant us love and gentleness.

Priest:

> Odin, our father, grant us knowledge and justice.

Priestess:

> Frigga, our mother, grant that our lives may be fruitful.

Priest:

> All goodly powers grant us blessing!

Priestess:

> Let us take this honey cake made in the shape of the sun. It represents the sun's powers of health, power, wealth, and joy. As we eat of it let us partake of the blessings of this Midsummer Day!

Priest:

> The rite is over. Let the feasting begin!

Druidic Rite for Midsummer

The ceremony should be performed at noon on the day of the summer solstice. The best place to perform it is on a hilltop or stone circle orientated to Midsummer.

The acting chief druid/druidess and the bard, who is also responsible for blowing the horn and for drumming when it is needed, perform the rite. A man dressed in gold and yellow and crowned with oak leaves represents the Sun Lord, while a woman dressed in green and crowned with flowers represents the Earth Mother. The other celebrants wear white, the druid color for Midsummer, and the women wear wreaths of flowers and the men wreaths of oak leaves.

A circle is set up with the altar in the center, and the cardinal points of north, east, south, and west are marked. This is decorated with greenery, including St. John's wort, fennel, birch, mugwort, and lavender.

Everyone, led by the druid, processes around the outside of the circle three times before stopping at the north East Point of the circle, which is the entry point.

Druid:

> *I ask all ye here assembled, Art thou ready to erect the sacred temple and celebrate the rites of Alban Heruin?*

Celebrants:

> *We are ready.*

All enter the circle and walking sunwise arrange themselves around it.

Druid: (traces the outline of the circle with the ceremonial sword)

> *I conjure thee, O circle of power, that thou beest a meeting place of love, joy, and truth, a shield against all wickedness and evil, a bulwark that shall contain all the power we raise within thee. In the names of the gods and goddesses we worship, so shall it be.*

Bard:

    Spirits of this place, hear us! Spirits of this place, we honor thee and ask thee to be with us in our rites.

Celebrants:

    Be with us!

Druid:

    We stand in awe beneath the Sky Father
    We stand in love upon the Earth Mother
    Druids gathered here to celebrate the rite of Alban Heruin,
    The rite of Midsummer, the rite of light on the water,
    The rite of the marriage of the Sun and the Earth
    The rite of awen, inspiration of bards and artists.

Bard:

    This is the longest day, the time of greatest light. The powers of winter are far away, the powers of darkness a story for children. We gather to celebrate in this time of brightness. We honor the Lord of the Sun and the Lady of the Earth, whose marriage causes the grain to grow, the vine to ripen, and the herbs to become imbued with power. Without their gifts we would not be.

Druid:

    I call upon the presence of the Great Lady, the Earth Goddess, the Mother of the Land. We gather here in her name to celebrate this festival of growth and fruitfulness.

The woman representing the Earth Goddess steps forward.

Earth Goddess:

    I am life, I am abundance
    I produce everything in Nature, I produce you, my children
    I bestow wealth, I bestow wisdom
    I am first in all things, I surround you
    I am beneath your feet
    I give you the food you eat, the water you drink
    From me come all you see, all that breathes

From me comes every word you hear
Those who do not honor me destroy themselves
Study me, listen to me
I am all pleasure, all life, all knowledge.

Druid:

    I call upon the presence of the Sun God, the great archer whose arrows are shafts
of light, the bright one, the all-seeing eye, the Lord of Light.

The man representing the Sun God steps forward.

Sun God:

    I am the bright and shining light,
I am the eye of the sky,
I see right through to the limits of the darkness
I behold everything, even into the realm of chaos
My blessings fall upon the earth and cause the crops to grow.

The druid takes the strongest hand of each and places them together, so that they stand hand in hand. He loops a red ribbon around their hands, but loosely and with no knots.

Druid:

    On this day of greatest light when the pregnant earth blossoms with flowers and
fruitfulness, we witness what the marriage of heaven and earth may achieve.

Earth Goddess:

    Come from the blazing heavens, my lover, my husband,
Come from the heavens, come!
Let me bathe in your light, my lover, my husband,
Let me rest in your arms.

Sun God:

    Open up your petals, like roses planted near running waters,
Send up a sweet scent like honeysuckle
Break forth in blossoms like the lily, yield fragrance,
Bring forth leaves in grace and praise in song.

Druid:

    Let us give reverence to the joining of the Sun God and the Earth Goddess. We honor and bless them!

All:

    We honor and bless them!

The bard offers the Earth Goddess a basket of green grain, unripe fruit, and a loaf of bread. She holds out her hands in blessing over it and says:

Earth Goddess:

    I bless the growing crops, the golden grain waving in the wind, the burgeoning fruit on the trees and vines, the roots in the earth, the stems and the buds. I bless the life in young animals and children. All this I bless in the name of the Goddess of the Earth, the mother of us all.

The Sun God extends his arms toward the sky.

Sun God:

    I bless the growing crops, the golden grain waving in the wind, the burgeoning fruit on the trees and vines, the roots in the earth, the stems and buds. I bless the life in young animals and children. All this I bless in the name of the Sun God, the father of us all.

Earth Goddess: (addressing the gathered celebrants)

    Remember, all of you, that you are stewards of my earth. When you abuse and defile it, you abuse and defile me. When you ravage the earth for its wealth, you rape and impoverish me. When you contaminate the earth, you poison me. Be my good stewards and ever honor and protect the land, as you would do honor to me. Dishonor me and you will feel my wrath in full measure. Be my good stewards and I shall reward you beyond imagining.

Sun God: (addressing all the celebrants)

    Remember, all of you assembled here, that you are the stewards of my gift of light and life. Always strive to bring light, healing, joy, and love into your own life and into the lives of others. Remember that you are my stewards, the protectors of my creatures, the animals, and all that is wild and free. Harm the least of these and you

harm me. Dishonor me and you will feel my wrath in full measure. Be my good stew-
ards and I shall reward you beyond imagining.

The druid steps forward and lights the prepared bonfire (or torch, if bonfires are not
suitable for the spot).

Druid:

Let the fire be lit, not only here on this Midsummer Day, but also in our hearts
and minds for all our lives!

All:

May the fire be lit!

Bard:

May Awen, the light of inspiration, descend and shine across the water!

All:

May Awen descend!

There is now a quiet time of meditation, while all wait for inspiration to descend, or
for prophecies and messages from the gods. Various types of divination may be
employed.

When all are ready, the fire is refreshed and fire jumping takes place as an act of
purification and renewal. Food is shared and the bard begins the sharing of poetry,
song, and verse with a poem relating to the season. Others may add what they have
learned during the time of meditation, sing a suitable song, recite a suitable verse,
or read a suitable passage relating to the season and its inspirations.

When all is finished, the druid pours a libation of wine to the Earth Mother (i.e.,
he or she pours some wine on the earth) and says:

Druid:

We give thanks to the Great Goddess of the Earth. Mother, grant us your bless-
ings. Grant us full orchards and fields of ripening grain. Be with us in our lives, as
you once were to those of old. Grant us your love and blessings. Let blessing be!

All:

Let blessing be!

Druid: (holding his arms to the heavens)

O Lord of the Sun, great eye of the heavens! Grant your light and your blessing to this land, protect us from the powers of blight and darkness. Be with us in our lives as you once were to those of old. Grant us your wisdom and your blessings. Let blessing be!

All:

Let blessing be!

The druid goes around the temple with the sword counterclockwise to wind down the power and close the temple.

Druid:

Together, brothers and sisters, we have met together to celebrate the rite of Midsummer. We have witnessed the marriage of the Sun God and the Earth Mother. We have heard their blessings and done them honor. The rite is ended, let us go in peace until we meet again.

All:

Go in peace!

Handfasting

A handfasting is a Pagan wedding, the union of two members of a group solemnized by the presiding priest and priestess. The term is an old Scottish one and referred to a trial marriage. In certain areas it was considered acceptable even

though frowned on by the Church. The custom goes back to ancient times when a couple would link hands through a holed stone and undertake a trial marriage for "a year and a day." If the relationship did not work, the couple would return to the stone and depart from it in different directions. Until recent times unmarried couples were referred to as "living over the brush," a reference to the fact that they had jumped over a broomstick to signify their intent to live together as a couple without the sanction of the church and state.

In modern Pagan practice, handfasting is a marriage bond undertaken for a year and a day or "as long as love shall last," rather than for a lifetime. In a time when we know that divorce is common, and for whatever reasons many relationships do not last a lifetime, it is perhaps a sensible option. The couple often renew their vows each year and follow the handfasting with a civil ceremony.

The period after the marriage is called the "honeymoon," from the practice of the ancient Teutons of drinking honey wine for thirty days after the marriage. Honey was widely believed to be an aphrodisiac in ancient and medieval times and was an indispensable ingredient of love potions and spells or was taken with food and wine.

The priest and priestess together, or the priestess alone, conduct the ceremony. The groom is accompanied by a groomsman—an old name for a best man. A bridesmaid accompanies the bride.

On the altar a cup is placed from which the couple will drink, then break, as a token that no other shall share what they have together. In addition, the two rings are placed on the book of rituals. Flowers such as meadowsweet, apple blossom, violets, cherry blossom, and roses are placed on the altar, about the circle and wreathed into chaplets for the couple and their guests.

The circle is decorated with seasonal flowers, which might include meadowsweet, violets, lavender, apple blossom, etc.

The circle is cast.

Priestess:
  I call upon (love goddess name),[14]
  the goddess of love.
  Lady of blessings, thee I invoke.
  Thou art the moment when body knits
  to body

And the world flowers.
You enliven everything: plants in the meadow
The fish in the sea, the creatures of the forest,
The birds tumbling on the wind.
Thou art our darling, thou who
Under the wheeling stars makes all things
Blossom and bear fruit.
At your approach the storm clears
Dark clouds dissolve to blue
The sweet earth and all the oceans smile
Your light dances brilliant
Through the flourishing world.

Groomsman:
There are those in our midst who seek the bonds of handfasting.

Priestess:
Let them be named and brought forward.

Groomsman: (bringing the groom forward)
(groom's name) *is the man.*

Bridesmaid: (bringing the bride forward)
(bride's name) *is the woman.*

Priestess: (to groom)
Are you (groom's name)?

Groom:
I am.

Priestess:
And what is your desire?

Groom:

> *To be made one with* (bride's name) *in the eyes of the Old Gods.*

Priest: (to bride)

> *Are you* (bride's name)?

Bride:

> *I am.*

Priest:

> *And what is your desire?*

Bride:

> *To be made one with* (groom's name) *in the eyes of the Old Gods.*

Priestess: (holds knife aloft)

> *Lord and Lady, here before you stand two of your people. Witness now that which they have to declare* (places the knife at the groom's chest). *Repeat after me:*
> *I,* (groom's name), *do come here of my own free will to seek the partnership of* (bride's name). *I come with all sincerity, wishing only to become one with her I love. Always will I strive for* (bride's name)'s *happiness and welfare. Her life will I defend before my own. May the athame be plunged into my chest should I not be sincere in all that I declare. All this I swear before the Lord and the Lady. May they give me the strength to keep my vows. So mote it be.*

Priest: (holds knife aloft)

> *Lord and Lady, here before you stand two of your people. Witness now that which they have to declare* (places the knife at the bride's chest). *Repeat after me:*
> *I,* (bride's name), *do come here of my own free will to seek the partnership of* (groom's name). *I come with all sincerity, wishing only to become one with him I love. Always will I strive for* (groom's name)'s *happiness and welfare. His life will I defend before my own. May the athame be plunged into my chest should I not be sincere in all that I declare. All this I swear before the Lord and the Lady. May they give me the strength to keep my vows. So mote it be.*

Rings are exchanged. A cup of wine is shared between the bride and groom, which they then break as a sign that no one else shall partake of what they share together.

Priestess:

> *Ever love, help, and respect each other, and know that you are one in the eyes of the Gods and the Craft.*

All:

> *So mote it be.*

The bride and the groom kiss each other, then the celebrant and sponsors. A broomstick is brought forward and the couple jumps over it. They then receive the congratulations of all and are showered in rose petals, rice, and orange blossoms. A feast or picnic follows. If you want to add personal statements, etc., into the rite, it is perfectly acceptable. After all, it is your day.

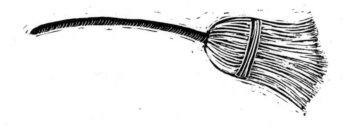

1. Many people do not begin the invocations until reaching the east, as this is the direction of vocalization.
2. Seasonal invocations of particular aspects of the God and Goddess may be substituted here.
3. Insert here the name your coven uses for the Goddess, or the name of goddess you wish to work with.
4. Insert here the name your coven uses for the God, or the name of the god you wish to work with.
5. This might be, "We come here to celebrate the festival of Midsummer."
6. Insert here the name your coven uses for the God.
7. This act symbolizes the marriage of heaven and earth.
8. Insert here the name your coven uses for the God.
9. Ibid.
10. Insert here the name your coven uses for the Goddess.
11. Ibid.
12. If this is not possible, you could take a candle in a jar around the fields or, lacking a field, around your garden or even a window box.
13. Anna Franklin, *The Sacred Circle Tarot* (St. Paul, MN: Llewellyn, 1998).
14. Insert here the name of the love goddess whom you feel most drawn to.

Appendix 1

Animal Totems for Midsummer

Bee

The Great Goddess is often pictured as a queen bee. Cybele was the queen bee for whom her priests castrated themselves to become her drones (as the drone is emasculated by the queen during mating); they were called the *melissae*, the "bees," as were the priestesses of Demeter. The officiates at the mysteries of Eleusis were also called *bees*. The Greek word for bee, *melissa*, gave its name to lemon balm, or *Melissa officinalis*, which, according to Pliny, attracts bees above all other plants.

Another favorite food of bees is heather. At Midsummer, Cybele, as queen bee, imprisoned Attis in heather. Osiris was also imprisoned in heather and freed by Isis, presumably also as queen bee. The Roman love goddess Venus courted Anchises on the mountainside to the hum of bees. The Greeks consecrated bees to the moon.

The honeybee orientates itself on its journey by the angle and position of the sun, and the Celts regarded it as a messenger who traveled the paths of sunlight to the realm of the spirits. Being winged, bees share with birds the ability to carry messages from this world to the world of spirits, and the old practice of telling the bees in the hive all the family news originated with sending messengers to souls in the Otherworld.

Butterfly

The summertime is the season of the butterfly. In Britain, Europe, North America, and the Pacific the butterfly was a symbol of the soul and attraction to the light. It was often thought that the human soul left the body in the form of a butterfly, and the creature was therefore treated with respect.

Butterflies appear in Celtic beliefs as Otherworld guides, perhaps as souls. Their names include *Dealan-de, Tarmach-de,* and *Dearbadan-de,* each containing the Scottish Gaelic for deity, *de.* In Russia they often appear as emblems of the soul, *Dushichka,* from *dusha,* or "soul." They share similar mythology in Central America.

Medieval angels and fairies are sometimes depicted with butterfly wings. Butterflies are the symbol of the Sidhe, and fairies are often pictured as riding on their backs. The Celts wore butterfly badges as a mark of respect for the ancestral spirits.

The transformation of the butterfly from egg to caterpillar to pupae to chrysalis to butterfly is seen as an allegory for death and rebirth. The Celts saw the butterfly as symbol of rebirth; at the festivals where all torches and lights were extinguished and relit from a central bonfire, the brand was called a "butterfly."

Bull

The bull is an ancient symbol of power, fertility, and strength, associated with kingship, the land, and the midsummer sun. Many gods and goddesses were described as keeping cattle. The Welsh sun god Hu had a bull called "the mighty Hu," while the sun god Beli was called "the loud-roaring Beli"; the bull is strong, fertile, and life giving, associating it with the sun. In Celtic myth the solar cart was pulled by three oxen, rather than horses. For the druids the bull was the sun and the cow the earth.

This is echoed in other mythologies, such as the mating of the Canaanite Baal and his sister in bull-and-cow form, the mating of the Greek sky god Zeus and Io in bull-and-cow form, and so on. In ancient Egypt the sacred Apis bull was worshipped at Memphis and treated as a living god. It was sacred to Ra, the sun god.

Black bulls are linked to the north, the winter solstice, and the underworld, while white bulls are linked with sky gods, the south, and the summer solstice.

The bull symbolizes the masculine, solar, generative forces of the sky gods. The human king, to align himself with the bull's divine power, often wore a bull's tail, hide, or curly beard. The bellow of the bull is reminiscent of thunder, and many old oak trees are known as bull oaks. Lightning strikes the oak more than any other tree, and oaks were particularly associated with the thunder god.

Cock

The cry of the rooster at sunrise indicates the end of the darkness and the start of the day. The Greeks believed that the rooster was sacred to Apollo, the sun god, and was associated with his son Asklepios, the healer god, through its association with the sun and its life-giving powers. In the cult of Mithras the rooster was a symbol of the sun god. It was the Orphic bird of resurrection. In the later druidic mysteries, the hen's egg, dyed red to represent the sun, took the place of the serpent's egg.

The crowing of the rooster is thought to drive away ghosts, darkness, and the powers of the night. The corn dolly was often made into the shape of a rooster, and these corn roosters were placed on top of the rick to protect them.

Cow

The cow is the symbol of plenty, nourishment, and nurture, associating it with mother goddesses. Nomadic and pastoral tribes regarded the cow as a symbol of life and fertility and they depended on it for food and prosperity. As such, it was a beast of the life-giving Goddess. The Greek sun and sky god Zeus was nursed by a cow. His wife Hera is described as "cow-eyed" (*boopis*) by Homer. In Celtic lore, Madron, the Great Mother, was also associated with the cow and is often depicted as a matronly woman holding a cornucopia (cow's horn) filled with fruit and grains. For the druids, the bull represented the fertilizing power of the heavens, while the cow represented the productive abundance of the earth.

Deer and Stag

The stag was one of the four sacred animals of the Celts and has played an important part in folklore in many areas of the world. The white stag may be seen as a solar symbol. Legends often tell of a stag fighting with a snake or underworld/winter animal, sometimes drawing it from the ground with its nostrils and then swallowing it or trampling it.

The stag is most closely associated with the Gaulish god Cernunnos, who wears stag horns. He is portrayed on the Gundestrup cauldron, dating from 300 B.C.E., as a seated figure with antlers growing from his head. He holds a snake in one hand and a torc in the other, showing that he is a god of winter and summer, sky and underworld, death and resurrection. The animals of the forest surround him.

Eagle

The power and strength of the eagle associate it with authority and royalty. The eagle is a solar symbol, representing both temporal and spiritual power. It soars upward into the heavens, wheeling on currents of air, the element of inspiration. It was thought that eagles could stare at the sun without blinking and that fledgling eagles would be taken close to the sun to stare at it as an initiation; those who blinked were unworthy and fell to their death. In Christian art the eagle is the emblem of St. John, as, like the eagle, he "looked on the glory of the sun." The Greeks and Romans thought the eagle was the only bird to be found in the heavens with the gods. It was the totem bird of Mithras and the messenger of Apollo. For the Aztecs the eagle was a solar power, the rising sun, the devourer of the serpent of darkness. As the traditional enemy of the serpent, the eagle is carved on church lecterns. For the Egyptians the eagle was the chief representative of the sun, Ra, and was said to descend in a shaft of light over the head of a pharaoh during his coronation.[1] In Celtic lore the eagle was also associated with sun gods and heroes. A pair of eagles carrying chains guards the grave of Arthur in Snowdonia. Llew adopted the form of an eagle and sat in an oak tree.

The eagle was thought to renew itself by flying to the sun and scorching its feathers before plunging into the sea to emerge as a young bird. It is a symbol of the resurrection of the spirit, renewal, and the power of life over death.

As a solar power it is in conflict with the powers of the underworld, represented by the snake. Some species of eagle eat serpents and can sometimes be seen carrying them. In Hittite myth the eagle with the serpent in its talons symbolized the strife between the weather god and the serpent Illuyankas. It is an expression of the tension between the sky and the underworld, between summer and winter, between light and darkness.

Falcon and Hawk

The hawk is associated with the sun in symbolism because of its flight, ferocity, and piercing, yellow eyes. The sparrowhawk was sacred to Horus in ancient Egypt and was associated with the east, the east wind, and the resurrected sun god who rises in the east. At the coronation of a pharaoh, a hawk (some say an eagle), as an emissary from the sun god Ra, was said to descend over the head of the pharaoh, just as a dove descended on Jesus as he was baptized by John.

The hawk was also a solar bird in Greece and Rome. The kite was sacred to the Greek sun god Apollo as Lord of the Delphic Oracle, because circling in the sky, it saw everything.

Goose

The goose is an important bird in European and Asian folklore. Wild geese are associated with the sun and sun gods. In China, too, the bird was a solar power, and signified the seasonal change to autumn and was depicted with the autumn moon. Among the Celts, the goose was a sacred solar bird, and eating its flesh was taboo, except at the Midwinter feast when a ritual meal of goose flesh was eaten.

Horse

Horses are symbolic of the sun, moon, and the land. They represent virility, fertility, strength, and swiftness. Horse cults existed in Britain long before the coming of the Celts and would have been centered on the wild ponies. A Stone Age carving found in Derbyshire shows a man in a horse mask. Even today there is a repugnance to eating horseflesh in Britain—a taboo that in ancient times would have been lifted in October, as with the October horse in Rome and the horse feast in Denmark.

In most ancient civilizations the sun was thought to be drawn across the sky by celestial horses. Several of these are named in myth, including Abraxas, a horse of the dawn goddess Aurora (the letters of his name in Greek make the numerical value 365, the number of days of the year); Aethon ("fiery red"), a sun horse; Eoos ("dawn"), another horse of Aurora; and Abakur ("hot one"). Dag, the Norse god of the day, was conveyed across the sky by his white horse, Shining Mane, which spread light across the world. Odin possessed an eight-legged horse named Sleipnir, who could run across land and water alike (eight is the number of solar increase). It carried Hermod to the underworld to beg Hel for the return of the slain Baldur.

Lizard

The lizard's name in Welsh (*Lleufer*) and Gaelic (*Bog-luachair*) associate it with light. The lizard is sun loving and is therefore associated with the sun. Lizards hibernate and reemerge in the spring. In Europe it was thought to go blind during the winter and emerge blind in the spring, when it climbs on an east-facing wall and looks east to the sunrise, and thus has its sight restored. In the east it is a symbol of overpowering heat, while in Egypt it was the symbol of fecundity, as its activity increases when the Nile floods, stimulating the return of life. In Polynesia the lizard is also associated with the sun and was thought to be a messenger of the gods, or even kin to them.

Reindeer

In Slavic and Scandinavian myth the sun chariot is sometimes pulled across the sky by reindeer, rather than horses. This is possibly where the myth of Father Christmas and his reindeer originates.

Snakes

Midsummer was the night when the serpents of Britain would roll themselves into a hissing, writhing ball called the *glain*, or "serpent's egg," "snake stone," or "druid's egg." According to other stories the serpent's egg is a glass ball or an ammonite fossil. In any case, anyone in possession of it could claim great magical powers.

Swan

The swan is associated with the sun, daughters of the sun, and it sometimes draws the sun chariot. All across Europe the swan is associated with the sun or daughters of the sun, and it sometimes draws the sun chariot. Swan maidens such as the Valkyrie have solar connections.

Woodpecker

The woodpecker is a bird of fecundity. Its Babylonian name means "Ax of Ishtar," Ishtar being the fertility goddess. It hammers its bill into the cracks of oak trees, often seen as an erotic metaphor, and this theme is echoed in folk songs throughout Europe. It climbs trees spirally and is therefore thought to be a bird of rebirth.

It announces nourishing summer rains by hammering its bill on oak trees and generally indicates storms. In France, Germany, Austria, and Denmark it is given names similar to its English name of "rain bird." In Italy there is a saying, "When the woodpecker pecks, expect a storm."

The woodpecker is associated with Zeus, the Greek sky and thunder god, who once changed himself into one. Pikus ("woodpecker"), son of Saturnus and father of Pan, was turned into a woodpecker by Circe for spurning her love.

---

1. Robert Graves, *The White Goddess* (London: Faber and Faber, 1965).

Appendix 2

Midsummer Calendar

This calendar is included so that you can see the buildup of themes toward the summer solstice and away again, moving toward Lughnasa. The date of the summer solstice can vary from June 19 to 23 in the Northern Hemisphere and December 19 to 23 in the Southern Hemisphere.

June 1

Sacred to Juno (Roman chief goddess)[1]
Feast of Syn (Nordic goddess)[2]
St. Wistan's Day[3]
St. Wite's Day[4]
Festival of Carnea

June 2
St. Elmo's Day[5]

June 3
Feast of Bellona (Roman goddess of war)

June 4
The Rosalia
St. Petroc's Day[6]

June 6
Feast of Hathor
Feast of Hecate
Feast of Artemis
Feast of Bendidia
St. Boniface's Day

June 7
Feast of Athene
Feast of Vesta
St. Meriasek's Day (patron saint of Cornish tin miners)
St. Colman's Day (an Ulster saint)

June 8
Feast of Bandi
Feast of Bendidia
St. William's Day[7]

June 9
Feast of Vesta
St. Columba's Day[8]

June 10
Feast of Anahita

June 11

Feast of Mater Matuta[9]
Feast of Concordia (Roman goddess of peace and harmony)
Feast of St. Barnabas[10]
Old Day of the Summer Solstice[11]

June 12

Feast of Maat

June 13

Nativity of the Muses
Feast of Minerva (Roman goddess of wisdom)
Feast of Epona (Celtic horse goddess)
Feast of Sul (Celtic goddess of healing water and wisdom)
Feast of the goddess Rosea
Festival of the Valkyries
Day of Women's Power
St. Antony's Day

June 14

Birthday of the Muses
Day of Vidar (patron of leather workers)[12]

June 15

Feast of Vesta, the Vestalia
Feast of Minerva
St. Vitus Day

June 17

Feast of Eurydice
St. Nectan's Day[13]
St. Botolph's Day[14]

June 18

Feast of Anna
Feast of Anu
Feast of Danu
Feast of the Norns
Feast of Fortuna

June 19

Feast of Hera
Feast of Juno
Feast of the White Buffalo Woman
Feast of St. Edmund

June 20

Day of the Pagan martyr Iron Skegge[15]
Solstice Eve
St. Govan's Day[16]
St. Alban's Day[17]

June 21

Summer Solstice
Feast of the Great Mother
Feast of Juno Luna
Feast of Hera, Queen of Heaven
Placation of Tempestas (Roman goddess of storms)
Feast of Cardea (Roman goddess of the hinges)[18]
Feast of Hebe the Cupbearer
Feast of Cerridwen (Welsh goddess of the cauldron)
Feast of Wadjet
Feast of Blodeuwedd (Welsh Lady of the Flowers)
Druidic Festival of Alban Heruin
Saxon Feast of Litha
Feast Day of Baldur (god of light in Norse myth)

June 22

In some years, the Summer Solstice
Feast of Cerridwen
St. Thomas Moore's Day

June 23

Midsummer Eve
St. John's Eve
Feast of Ishtar and Tammuz
Feast of the Cornish Lady of the Flowers

June 24

Midsummer Day
St. John's Day
Mannannan's Day[19]
Feast of the Swedish Midsummer Bride
Feast of Fors Fortuna ("Lady Luck")
Feast of Venus
Feast of Aphrodite
Feast of Ishtar
Feast of Astarte
Festival of Vesta
Feast of the Rosa Mundi ("Rose of the World")
Well-Dressing Day

June 25

St. Non's Day[20]
Feast of Shakti
Feast of Ishtar
Feast of Kali Ma
Feast of Ceridwen

June 26

Feast of the Spider Woman
Feast of Gaia (Greek earth goddess)
St. Anne's Day
Cherry harvest fairs

June 27

Initium Aestatis, Feast of Aestas (Roman goddess of summer)
Beginning of Roman summertime

June 28

Feast of Hemera
St. Peter's Eve

June 29

St. Peter's and St. Paul's Day[21]
Beginning of the Runic Year with the rune Feoh[22]
Sacred to Frey and Freya
Rushbearing Day
Old St. John's Day

June 30

Feast of Gaia
Feast of Aestas

July 3

Beginning of the Dog Days (rise of Dog Star, Sirius)
Sacred to Loki (Norse god of fire and mischief)[23]

July 4

Old Midsummer Eve[24]
Little St. John's Day

July 5

Old Midsummer Day

July 7

Feast of Consus (Roman god of the harvest)

---

1. In Roman lore the whole month is sacred to Juno, Queen of Heaven. She is the guardian of women, so June is the most propitious month for marriage. She also appears this month as Juno Moneta, who rules wealth, and this is the most favorable month for material gain.
2. In Norse lore the month is called the *Fallow Month*, because this is the time when hay is ready.
3. St. Wistan was a Saxon prince murdered for his opposition to his cousin's incestuous relationship with the queen of Mercia.
4. St. Wite is an obscure saint with a tomb at Whitchurch Canonicorum in Dorset, England. Those seeking healing make offerings of cake and cheese there.
5. Nothing is known about this alleged saint, who gave his name to St. Elmo's fire, the glow resulting from electrical discharge seen around ship's masts or church steeples. In Pagan terms, this phenomenon was important at this time of year, symbolizing fire from the heavens being brought to earth.
6. St. Petroc is the patron saint of Cornwall. He was a sixth-century Cornishman who founded monasteries in Padstow and Little Petherick. In recent years this has become a day of celebration for those proud of their Cornish heritage.
7. Twelfth-century Archbishop of York.
8. An Irish missionary who established a monastery on Iona.
9. The festival of the Roman dawn goddess Mater Metuta. Women led female servants to her temple, and then beat them with sticks.
10. St. Barnabas is often pictured carrying a hat rake, since this is the time when hay making ("Haysel") begins.
11. Before the calendar was changed, when eleven days were added into the year to correct a cumulative misalignment of seasons, June 11 was the day of the summer solstice.
12. According to Norse lore, Vidar is a son of Odin, who survives Ragnarok.
13. In England, wells were dressed with foxgloves in honor of St. Nectan, who was associated with a well at Hartland Point and a waterfall in Cornwall. Nectan was actually a Celtic god, and the well-dressing is an old Pagan rite.
14. St. Botolph may be another saintly candidate with a Pagan origin. He is a kind of gatekeeper or doorkeeper, one of the great themes of the month. He is said to have done battle with the devil, and the town of Boston in Lincolnshire, England, is named after him (a contraction of "Botolph's town"). How many people in Boston, Massachusetts (in the United States), know that?
15. Iron Skegge was tortured to death by the Christian King of Norway, Olaf Tryggvason.

16. St. Govan is said to have lived in a chapel in Wales during the Dark Ages, but here is another Pagan god in disguise as a Christian saint. He has been Sir Gawain, a knight of King Arthur, but it is more likely that he is the Celtic smith god Govan or Goibniu. It is said that if you stand inside a fissure in his chapel and make a wish on this day, you will gain your heart's desire.

17. A rose ceremony is held at St. Alban's Cathedral in England. Children carry roses to the saint's shrine.

18. Cardea is the Roman goddess of hinges, the includer and excluder. On this day doors and windows should be maintained magically.

19. At Barrule on the Isle of Man, bundles of grass were laid down for the Celtic god Mannannan, the patron deity of the island. This custom went on well into the nineteenth century. He was said to appear on Midsummer Day in the form of a heron, sometimes in order to woo a mortal lover.

20. At St. Non's Well in Cornwall, England, lunatics can be cured by pushing them into the well and then tossing them up and down.

21. In many places the festivities begun on St. John's Eve went on until St. Peter's and St. Paul's Day.

22. Nigel Pennick and Helen Field, *The God Year* (Chieveley: Capall Bann, 1998).

23. The Dog Star Sirius is called "Loki's brand."

24. Owing to the calendar changes of 1752, the date of Midsummer moved. Some people, however, refused to alter their celebrations, and continued to celebrate on the old day. At Whalton, in Northumberland, England, the famous baal fires are still held. There is a great bonfire, morris dancers, fiddlers and pipers, and leaping the flames.

Appendix 3

Midsummer Correspondences

Names of the Midsummer/Summer Solstice Festival

Lá Fhéile Eoin (Irish)
An Fhéill-Eoin (Irish)
Gwyl Ifan (Welsh)
Golowan (Welsh)
Gouel Sant Yann (Breton)
Laa l'Ean (Manx)
Alban Hefin/Alban Heruin (modern Druid)
Coamhain (Celtic Pagan)
Litha (Saxon?)
Rasa (contemporary Lithuanian Paganism)

Ligo (Baltic)
Johnmas (Orkney)
St. John's Day (Christian)
St. Ivan's Day (Russian)
Beltane (parts of Ireland)
Johannisnacht (German)
Kesäjuhlat (Finnish)
Feast of Jean Baptiste (Canada)
Night of Vervain (Spanish)

Full Moon Nearest to the Summer Solstice

The nearest full moon to the summer solstice has a variety of names in Pagan tradition. According to folklore the Midsummer moon causes madness.

Dyad Moon
Lovers Moon
Mead Moon
Strawberry Moon
Oak Moon

Names of the Month of June

June (Modern English, named after the Roman goddess Juno)
The Fallow Month (Norse)
Equos—the Horse Month (Celtic Coligny calendar)
Meitheamh (modern Irish)
Mehefin (Welsh)
Metheven (Cornish)
Mezheven (Breton)
The Door of the Year (English magical tradition)

Midsummer Symbols

Sun wheels
Sun
Fire

Bonfires
Roses
Rosettes
Daisies
All rayed flowers
Herbs
Equal-armed crosses
Torches

Midsummer Colors

White (druidic color for the festival)
Red
Yellow
Gold
All colors of the sun and flames

Midsummer Gems

Tiger's-eye
Clear quartz
Topaz
Amber

Midsummer Tools

Wand
Cauldron
Spear

Midsummer Rune

Dag, the rune of opening. According to Nigel Pennick this represents the good door that lets in the beneficial, but keeps out the negative.[1]

Midsummer Ogham

Duir, the oak. Duir means "oak" or "door."

Basic Midsummer Energies

Power
Creativity
Inspiration
Love
Divination
God energy
Healing
Fertilization

---

1. Nigel Pennick, *Runic Astrology* (Wellingborough: Aquarian Press, 1990).

Appendix 4

Gods and Goddesses of Midsummer

Aestas—The Roman goddess of summer to whom this time is sacred.

Agni—Hindu fire god, son of the sky god and earth mother. His lightning brings fertilizing rain to the earth.

Aine or Ainé—Áine is an Irish goddess noted for her habit of taking mortal lovers. The hill of Cnoc Aine in County Limerick is her dwelling place, where she is still supposed to live as a fairy. She is said to have given the meadowsweet its scent. Her name means "brightness," "heat," or "speed," indicating that she is a sun goddess, and the word *Ain* is cognate to the Latin *ignis*, meaning "fire." Her festival is Midsummer, marked by a torchlight procession about her hill led by young women and a bonfire vigil. Her other title is Lair Derg, meaning "red mare," establishing her as a horse goddess, possibly cognate with the Welsh Rhiannon. Her festival celebrates the height of the sun's power, and farmers carried torches of straw and waved them over animals and fields for protection and fruitfulness, a way of carrying the sun's blessing of prosperity through fire.

Amaterasu—Japanese sun goddess from whom the royal family claims descent. Her brother is the moon god Tsukiyomi. She weaves the garments of the gods. Her symbols are cocks, kites, and heavenly arrows.

Amaunet—Egyptian goddess, a queen of heaven and wife of Amun.

Amun-ra—Egyptian sun god (see also *Ra*).

Anat—Canaanite fertility goddess who took the form of a cow to mate with her brother Baal in the form of a bull. This symbolizes the marriage of sky and earth.

Anu—In Irish lore the mother of the gods, possibly identical with Aine and Danu. An earth and fertility goddess. The twin hills at Killarney in Munster, Ireland, are called the "Paps of Anu."

Aphrodite—Greek goddess of love, born of the foam of the sea. Her festival is celebrated on June 24, and this day is propitious for love magic and divination.

Apollo—Greek and Roman god of the sun, healing, poetry, prophecy, and music. His sister Artemis is the moon goddess. He is the son of Zeus and Leto and the father of the god of medicine Asklepios.

Arani—A Hindu goddess of fire whose symbol is the wheel or swastika.

Arinna—Hittite sun goddess, married to the weather god. The king and queen enacted their annual sacred marriage. Only under her patronage could the rulers flourish. The sun disk or torch represented her.

Arthur—While there are legends of a British war leader named Arthur, many elements of the story may lead us to suppose that he was a death and resurrection god, most likely a solar deity.

Astarte—Canaanite goddess of fertility and love.

Athene—Greek warrior goddess of wisdom, celebrated at the summer solstice. She is the patroness of heroes, architects, spinners, and weavers.

Aurora—In Roman myth, "the rosy-fingered dawn." Her Greek equivalent is Eos.

Baal—Phoenician god of fertility, storms, and vegetation. His name simply means "Lord." Some speculate that the name of the Midsummer baal fires may relate to him, though this etymology is difficult to prove.

Baldur—A god of the Northern tradition called "the bright" or "the good god" or sometimes "the bleeding god." The light god who is born at the winter solstice and is killed at Midsummer. After his Midsummer sacrifice he descends into the underworld and waits to be reborn. His name relates to the Old English word *baeldar,* meaning "Lord," and for this reason he is compared to the Greek Adonis ("Lord") and the Slavic god Belbog, "the white shining one," the bringer of day.[1] Baldur's mother is Frigga, goddess of sexual love, and she traveled the world getting oaths from all things—plants, animals, spirits, gods, metals, rocks, etc.— that they would not harm her son, who had had a premonition of death. However, the trickster god Loki discovered that the humble mistletoe plant had not made such a promise, and fashioned a dart from it. He then organized a game in which all the gods amused themselves by harmlessly throwing all manner of things at Baldur. Loki persuaded Baldur's brother, the blind god Hoder ("hood"), to throw the dart at his twin. Thinking it harmless, Hoder agreed. The dart struck and Baldur fell dead. All the gods fell into grief and mourning. Odin sent a messenger to Hel, the goddess of the underworld, to ask what ransom she would take to return Baldur to them. She replied that if all living creatures wept for him, then he would be returned. All complied, except an old hag living in a cave—actually Loki in disguise.

Baldur may be identified with his near-namesakes Baal, Beli, Béél, and Bale. He is a god of light, a solar hero who struggles against the darkness. He and his consort Nanna are paralleled by the Celtic Beli and Anna, from whom Celtic nobility claim descent.

Barbale—Georgian sun goddess. Her name relates to the words for *wheel, circle,* and *blaze.* Women, who keep its matters secret, practice her cult. The Christians transformed her into St. Barbara.

Barbet—The sun goddess in Holland. St. Barbara absorbed many of her attributes.

Bast—Egyptian cat-headed goddess who represents the beneficent power of the sun.

Bel—Babylonian sun god mentioned in the Old Testament.

Belinos—Celtic sun god, patron of solar healing and renewal. The herbs of Midsummer are under his auspices; he causes them to grow. Those with yellow and gold flowers are particularly potent in this regard.

Blodeuwedd—"Flower Face." A Welsh goddess created by the magicians Math and Gwydion from nine types of flowers as a bride for Lleu Llaw Gyffes. She was unfaithful to him with Gronw and caused his death. As a punishment she was changed into an owl. Though some see her as the archetypal rebellious woman,[2] she is in fact the blossoming earth goddess in the summer, and her two lovers are summer and winter, or the gods of the waxing and waning sun.

Bochica—Columbian sun god who taught the Chibchas agriculture and the arts.

Brigit/Brighid—In Celtic legend Brighid is the daughter of the good god Dagda and was the Celtic counterpart of Athene. She is a triple fire goddess and her name comes from *Breo-saigit*, which means "fiery arrow." Hers are the three fire arrows (rays of the sun) of awen, inspiration, healing, and the hearth or forge. She is the muse of poets who lived under her patronage and who carried a golden branch hung with small bells in her honor. She is the goddess of healing wells where offerings were left to solicit healing. She is also a goddess of the hearth fire and the forge, patroness of the magician-smith who, by his alchemy, transforms elements of the underworld into beautiful or useful objects. Brighid is depicted with three objects: the mirror, the spinning wheel, and the cup or grail. Brighid is also known as the White Swan, a solar symbol, and she has several stations and festivals throughout the year, not just at Imbolc.

Cardea/Carnea—A Roman goddess, guardian of the hinges, of the home. She is a turning-of-the-year goddess in charge of the four winds.

Cerridwen—Welsh mother/moon/harvest goddess. She brewed the cauldron of knowledge, which contained all the wisdom of the world. The boy Gwion stole three drops. Ceridwen pursued him in a variety of shape-changing forms, finally eating him as a grain of corn. Nine months later he was born as Taliesin, the poet. This story is interpreted as a parable of initiation.

Chasca—An Inca flower goddess and attendant of the sun god. She is identified with the planet Venus.

Concordia—Roman goddess of peace and harmony, whose festival falls in June.

Cybele—Phrygian goddess of the earth. She was associated with the bee and was worshipped on mountain tops.

Danu—An Irish goddess, the mother of the Tuatha dé Danaan, which literally translates as "the People of the Goddess Danu." She is the daughter of the Dagda and is sometimes identified with Anu. The goddess Danu is probably Indo-European in origin and may be cognate with the Sanskrit water goddess Dánu ("The Flowing One").[3] Her name is found in the names of several rivers, such as the Danube. Dôn, the mother of a race of warriors, parallels her in Welsh literature. Originally a river goddess, she took on the attributes of a sovereign goddess of the land.

Daphne—In Greek myth, a nymph who was pursued by the sun god Apollo. She prayed to the gods to help her escape. They took pity by turning her into a bay tree. Her name means "the bloody one," and she is a goddess of the dawn who paints the sky red as she flees from the rising sun.

Donar—Teutonic thunder god cognate with Thor.

Epona—Horse/mother goddess of the Gauls and the British.

Erce—Old English earth goddess.

Erzulie—Haitian love goddess.

Flora—Roman flower goddess, especially associated with the rose.

Fortuna—A Roman fate goddess.

Frey—Scandinavian god of fertility. His chariot was drawn by boars.

Freya—"Lady." Teutonic goddess of the moon, love, and spring. She rides in a chariot drawn by cats.

Frigg/Frigga—Teutonic goddess of marriage and fruitfulness. The wife of Odin. Her name is still English slang for the sexual act.

Gaia—Greek earth goddess who created the universe.

Goibniu—Irish smith god, the uncle of Lugh.

Govan—June 20 is St. Govan's Day. His chapel is in Wales. He has been identified with Sir Gawain, coming there to live as a hermit after collapse of the Round Table, but is more likely to relate to Govannon. If you stand inside the rock cleft in the chapel on this day and make a wish, all your wishes and hopes will come true within the year as long as you are decisive about your wishes and turn around when you make them.

Govannon—Welsh smith god, cognate with Goibniu.

Grainne—Possibly a Celtic sun goddess of the waning year. She was promised in marriage to the old Finn, but she fell in love with the young Diarmuid. With drugged mead she put Finn and her father to sleep and ran away with her lover. They traveled the countryside, sleeping in a different cave each night, pursued by Finn for a year and a day, before they settled. After sixteen years Finn caught them and sent a boar to gore Diarmuid to death. She may be a form of Grian, the sun, and perhaps Finn ("white") is the moon. The year and a day is the solar year. Her name means "hateful," perhaps the hateful winter sun that withholds warmth.

Grian—Celtic goddess, sister of Aine. Her name means "sun." She lives at Cnoc Gréne in County Limerick. She represents the winter sun, perhaps to her sister Aine's summer sun.

Hadad—Babylonian thunder god who brought the fertilizing rain.

Hathor—Egyptian, cow-headed sky goddess of love, joy, and harmony.

Helios—Greek sun god, brother of the moon goddess Selene.

Hera—Greek queen of heaven and wife of the sky god Zeus.

Hestia—Greek goddess of the hearth fire. Her Roman equivalent is Vesta.

Hiribe—"The Summer King." A Hittite god and father of Nikkal, the goddess of the fruits of the earth.

Hoder/Hodur—The dark, blind, twin brother of Baldur, the Scandinavian god of light. The dark god who is killed at the winter solstice and is reborn at Midsummer.

Hu—Welsh sun god who kept a herd of bulls, animals that are always associated with sky/solar gods.

Hyperion—An early Greek prototype sun god, son of Gaia and Uranus. He is the father of Helios, the sun god.

Iarila—"Ardent Sun." Russian goddess whose festival was the summer solstice, celebrated with fire and water. Her brother was Iarilo and they mated together. Effigies of both of them were burned at Midsummer. He is shown as a youth in white, riding a horse. She appears in white, carrying flowers and riding a horse. She carries a sheaf of grain while girls sing and dance around her. Russian variants on her and her brother include Lado, Lada, Kupalo, and Kupal'nitsa, Christianized as Mary and Ivan—the summer solstice is St. Ivan's (John's) Day. At the summer solstice the god Kupalo and his consort were worshipped by young girls dressed as brides who processed down to the riverbank where they jumped up and down, just as the sun goddess jumps when she meets her husband, the moon. Homes were purified with sprinkled water.

Inanna—Sumerian queen of heaven and goddess of love, grain, weaving, and battle. A goddess of sovereignty whom the king had to "marry" in order to rule.

Indra—Hindu god of thunder and rain.

Ishtar—Assyrian mother goddess of love, fertility, battle, storms, the earth, and the moon.

Janicot—Basque witch god of the oak.

Janus—Roman god of the doorway and the turn of the year. He has two faces and looks back to what is past, and forward to see what is to come.

Jumala—Finno-Ugric oak and sky god.

Juno—Roman queen of heaven, wife of the sky god Jupiter, patroness of marriage and women.

Jupiter—Roman chief god, a god of the sky, thunder, rain, and storms.

Knowee—Australian Aboriginal sun goddess who circles the world holding a torch.

Kupalo—A Slavonic god of joy who is celebrated at Midsummer by gathering dew and bathing in streams and rivers. However, at the end of the festivities an image of him is thrown into the water, showing him also to be a sacrificed god.

Lleu Llaw Gyffes—"Lleu Strong Hand." A Welsh god with solar attributes. The son of Arianrhod, the moon goddess.

Lugh—An Irish god, sometimes called *Lugh Long Arm,* who is skilled in many crafts and has some solar attributes.

Macha—Irish war and horse goddess. A goddess of sovereignty to whom the sacred king would be wedded.

Marduk—Assyrian sun god and consort of Ishtar.

Maui—Polynesian sun god. His sister is Sina, goddess of the moon.

Mithras—Persian god of light, a god of the sun and victory. His cult spread with the soldiers of the Roman Empire and almost became the state religion in place of Christianity.

Nyame—Ashanti god of the sky, storms, and lightning.

Odin—Scandinavian chief god of war, knowledge, magic, and poetry. He is married to Frigg.

Perun—Slavonic god of the sun, lightning, and war. He was also a harvest god.

Pushan—Hindu sun god.

Ra—An Egyptian sun god who became subsumed to Amun as Amun-Ra. He emerged from the primordial waters in a lotus bud and gave birth to the gods of the sky and earth. He created the universe and humankind, called "the tears of Ra."

Rhiannon—Welsh horse/fertility goddess. Her name means "Great Queen."

Rosea—Roman rose goddess. June 24 is the festival of *rosa mundi* ("rose of the world").

Saule—The Baltic sun goddess. She formed the world from an egg after warming it for many years. At night she goes into the underworld in the west. Her daughter is the dawn. She is married to the moon. She dances on a stone in the middle of the sea on Midsummer Eve. On Midsummer Eve people stayed up all night hoping to see her dance as she came over the horizon at dawn. She helps women in childbirth and punishes evildoers. She can grant good health. She will not shine if there is too much evil about.

Shamash—Assyro-Babylonian sun god, the son of the moon god and earth goddess. His sister was Inanna. A torch represents him.

Shango—Nigerian thunder god.

Sól—In Norse myth the sun chariot was driven by Sól, while her brother Manu drove the chariot of the moon. Every dawn her chariot arises from the heavens and drives across the sky. At dusk it descends into the underworld. She is also called *Alfrodull* ("Elf Beam") or *Glory of the Elves*,[4] and is possibly the leader of the Light Elves. She married Dag, the god of day. Her totems include the wheel and the bronze chariot. When the end of the world approaches, she will grow pale and eventually will be devoured by the wolf Skoll.

Solntse—Russian sun goddess. She lives in a palace with gates in the east and west. She dwells there with the moon, her husband. They are married on Midsummer Day. People were buried at sunset so that they could make their journey to the underworld in the company of the goddess.

Sul—The goddess of springs at the city of Bath in southern England, she represents both fire and water. She rules healing waters. The Celts built a shrine around her spring and the Romans enlarged it into baths and a temple and called her *Sul Minerva* or *Minerva Medica*. She is depicted as a matronly woman with an owl beneath her foot, wearing a hat. A perpetual fire was kept burning at her temple. She was a patroness of weaving, spinning, and healing. Her name can mean either "sun" or "eye," or perhaps "burning" or "shining."[5]

Sunna—This German goddess is similar to the Norse Sol. In the evening she sits on a golden throne, and at dawn she simply stands up. Like many sun deities she is associated with spinning. She spins her sunbeams in the hour before sunrise. In Old English the word for sun, *sunne*, is feminine. Her feast day was probably Sunday, as the word incorporates her name. Pointing at the sun or sweeping toward her is unlucky.

Surya—A Hindu sun god who punishes evil and rewards good. People pray to him for healing.

Syn—The Norse goddess called "the includer and excluder," a goddess of boundaries, equivalent to the Roman Cardea. This is the time to maintain door hinges in her honor.

Taranis—Gaulish and British thunder god, whose symbols are the wheel and the lightning flash.

Tellus Mater—"Earth Mother." An early Roman earth/fertility goddess.

Tempestas—Roman storm goddess who must be placated at this time.

Tezcatlipoca—"Smoking Mirror." Aztec sun god, particularly the god of the summer sun.

Thor—Scandinavian sky and thunder god, the son of Odin. With his magic hammer he breaks up the winter ice each spring. He gave his name to Thursday.

Thunar—Anglo-Saxon thunder god, a god much venerated by the common people, like his Scandinavian counterpart Thor.

Tina—Etruscan thunder and fire god, the chief god of the Etruscan pantheon. The striking of his thunderbolts marked a place as sacred.

Tlaloc—Aztec thunder, rain, and mountain god.

Tonatiuh—Aztec sun god. His home was called the *House of the Sun* and was the abode of warriors.

Ukko—Finno-Ugric sky, thunder, and air god. He causes the rain to fall.

Upulero—Indonesian sun god.

Uttu—Sumerian sun god, cognate with the Babylonian Shamash.

Vesta—"Torch." Roman goddess of the hearth fire and ritual fire. A perpetual flame was kept burning by her priestesses, the Vestal Virgins. One of her festivals falls on June 24, though her chief festival, the Vestalia, fall on June 7.

Vishnu—Vedic sun god who had nine incarnations.

Woden—Anglo-Saxon chief god of war, knowledge, magic, and poetry.

Wotan—German chief god of war, knowledge, magic, and poetry.

Xochiquetzal—Aztec goddess of the moon, flowers, love, marriage, dancing, spinning, and weaving. She is the wife of the thunder god.

Yhi—Australian Aboriginal sun goddess, the great mother who created her husband and then all the animals and humankind.

Zeus—Greek chief god of the sky and thunder. He brings the fertilizing rains.

---

1. Mike Howard, "Baldur the Bright," *Talking Stick* (periodical, Spring, 1994).
2. Like Eve, created from the rib of Adam.
3. Dáithí Ó HÓgáin, *The Sacred Isle* (Woodbridge: Boydell Press, 1999).
4. Sheena McGrath, *The Sun Goddess* (London: Blandford, 1997).
5. Ibid.

Appendix 5

Sun Symbols

Circles and Discs

The sun is depicted as a circle in the petroglyphs of northern Europe. It is perhaps the most basic sun symbol of all. We see the sun as a flat circle from the vantage point of the Earth.

Crosses and Swastikas

Equal-armed crosses are solar symbols representing the four solar festivals and the turning of the year. Celtic crosses originally had nothing to do with Christianity. Brighid's crosses, made in the fashion of corn dollies, also appear in this connection.

The swastika is a related symbol, shown with ends on the arms of the cross to denote movement. They were originally Hindu and Scandinavian good-luck symbols, but have become so debased by their association with Nazism that it is doubtful whether their beneficial aspects can ever be reclaimed.

Eye

The sun is sometimes said to be the great eye of heaven. There are a large number of one-eyed gods who can be identified as sun gods. The sun sees all that happens on Earth, and its light uncovers all mysteries, which is why sun gods are associated with divination and oracular shrines.

Gold

This is the solar metal, bearing its color and brilliance.

Rayed Circles

Rays extending from the circle represent its beams of light.

Rosettes and Roses

Sun goddesses and the sun itself are often represented by the symbol of the rose, which, after all, flowers at Midsummer. The red color is also suggestive of fire.

Ships

Sometimes the sun disk is thought to travel across the sky on a ship.

Spinning Wheel

The Goddess is sometimes thought to have spun the world and to spin the rays of the sun each morning on her spinning wheel. Many goddesses associated with the sun and fire are also associated with spinning, as are a great number of fairies.

Spirals

These denote the sun's path through the year, inward to death and outward again to rebirth.

Wheels

The sun was often thought to wheel or roll through the sky, or to be a chariot drawn through the sky by horses. Therefore the wheel represents the movement of the sun. This gave rise to the custom of rolling burning wheels down hills at the summer solstice to bless areas with the sun's power.

Glossary

Athame—A witch's black-handled knife, used in ritual to invoke the circle.

Axis mundi—"Axis of the world." An imaginary or magically invoked pole that links a place or person to the realms of heaven, earth, and the underworld.

Coven—A group of witches or Wiccans.

Covener—A member of a coven.

Divining rod—A forked stick used to dowse water, metals, and other things.

Druid—A priest or priestess of the ancient Celts.

Hag—The crone or old-woman aspect of the Goddess, often representing winter.

Handfasting—A Pagan wedding, which binds a couple for "a year and a day."

Hieros Gamos—Sacred marriage of the God and Goddess, or the priest and priestess representing them.

Lustral—Consecrated water used for rituals of purification.

Ogham—A magical alphabet based on tree lore of the ancient Celts.

Rune—A magical alphabet of the Saxons and Norse.

Sidhe—Gaelic for *fairy*.

Torc—A Celtic, horseshoe-shaped necklace worn by chiefs and kings to denote their status.

Web—A magical concept that proposes that all things are linked in some way. Any action will resonate throughout the entire web.

Wiccan—A person who follows one of the magical traditions originating from Gerald Gardner, based on ancient witchcraft.

Wildfolk—British Craft term for *fairy folk*.

Witch—A practitioner of an ancient Pagan religion and magic.

Bibliography

Alcock, L. *Arthur's Britain*. London: Allan Lane, 1971.

Anderson, W. *Holy Places in the British Isles*. London: Ebury Press, 1983.

Anderson, William. *Green Man*. London: Harper Collins, 1990.

Aubrey, John. *Miscellanies*. 1696. Reprint, London: Reeves and Turner, 1890.

————. *Remaines of Gentilisme and Judaisme*. London, 1686.

Baker, Margaret. *Folklore and Customs of Rural England*. David and Charles, Newton Abbot, 1974.

Balfour, M. C. *Legends of the Cars*. London: Folk-Lore II, 1891.

Bancroft, Anne. *Origins of the Sacred*. London: Arkana, 1987.

Bellingham, David. *Celtic Mythology*. London: Apple Press, 1990.

Bett, Henry. *English Legends*. London: B. T., Batsford, 1950.

Billson, Charles. *County Folk-lore I: Leicestershire and Rutland*. London: Folklore Society, 1895.

Black, G. F. *County Folk Lore Vol. III Orkney and Shetland Islands*. London: Folklore Society, 1901.

———. *County Folk-lore III: Orkney & Shetland Islands*. London: Folklore Society, 1903.

Blamires, Steve. *The Irish Celtic Magical Tradition*. London: Aquarian Press, 1992.

Bord, Janet and Colin. *The Secret Country*. London: Paladin, 1978.

Bottrell, W. *Traditions and Hearthside Stories of West Cornwall*. Penzance, 1870.

Branston, Brian. *The Lost Gods of England*. London: Thames and Hudson, 1957.

Brewer. *Dictionary of Phrase and Fable*. Leicester: Blitz Editions, 1990.

Brewer, E. *Dictionary of Phrase and Fable*. London: Cassell and Co., 1885.

Bulfinch, Thomas. *Bulfinch's Mythology*. New York, NY: Modern Library, 1991.

Caldecott, Moyra. *Women in Celtic Myth*. Vermont: Destiny Books, 1992.

Campbell, Joseph. *The Way of Animals Powers*. London: Times Books, 1984.

Carmichael, Alexander. *Carmina Gadelica*. Edinburgh: Oliver and Boyd, 1928.

Carr-Gomm, Phillip. *The Elements of the Druid Tradition*. Shaftsbury: Element Books, 1991.

Cavendis, R. *Legends of the Worlds*. London: Orbis, 1982.

Chetwynd, Tom. *A Dictionary of Sacred Myth*. London: Mandala Books, 1986.

Child, F. J. *The English and Scottish Popular Ballads*. London, 1882.

Clark, A., ed. *The Shires Ballads*, "The Mery Life of the Countriman." Oxford, 1907.

Coghlan, Ronan. *The Encyclopædia of Arthurian Legends*. Shaftsbury: Element Books, 1991.

Cooke, Ian. *Journey to the Stones*. Men an Tol: Men-an-Tol Studio, 1987.

Cooper, J. C. *Symbolic and Mythological Animals*. London: Aquarian Press, 1992.

———. *Symbolism*. Wellingborough: Aquarian Press, 1982.

Cooper, Quintin, and Paul Sullivan. *Maypoles, Martyrs and Mayhem*. London: Bloomsbury, 1994.

Courtney, Margaret. *Cornish Feasts and Folklore*. London, 1890.

Croker, T. Crofton. *Fairy Legends and Traditions of the South of Ireland*. London: John Murray, 1826.

Crossley-Holland, Kevin. *Folk Tales of the British Islands*. London: Folio Society, 1985.

———. *Norse Myths*. London: A. Deutsch, 1890.

Dixon-Kennedy, Mike. *Celtic Myth and Legend*. London: Blandford, 1997.

Douglas, George. *Scottish Fairy and Other Folk Tales*. Scott Publishing, 1893.

Durdin-Robertson, L. *The Year of the Goddess*. Wellingborough: Aquarian Press, 1990.

Ellis, P. B. *A Dictionary of Irish Mythology*. London: Constable, 1987.

Erbe, T., ed. *Mirk's Festival*. Early English Text Society, 1905.

Evans, J. G., ed. *The White Book of the Mabinogion*. Pwllheli, 1907.

Farrar, Janet and Stewart. *Eight Sabbats for Witches*. London: Robert Hale, Ltd., 1981.

———. *The Witches' God*. London: Robert Hale, 1989.

———. *The Witches' Goddess*. London: Robert Hale, 1987.

Franklin, Anna. *Familiars: The Animal Powers of Britain*. Chieveley: Capall Bann, 1997.

———. *The Sacred Circle Tarot*. St. Paul, MN: Llewellyn Publishing, 1998.

Franklin, Anna, and Sue Lavender. *Herb Craft*. Chieveley: Capall Bann, 1995.

Franklin, Anna, and Sue Phillips. *Pagan Feasts*. Chieveley: Capall Bann, 1997.

Frazer, J. G. *The Golden Bough*. 1922. Reprint, London: Macmillan, 1957.

Gantz, Jeffrey, trans. *Mabinogion*. London: Penguin, 1977.

Geoffrey of Monmouth. *The History of the Kings of Britain*. Trans. Lewis Thorpe. London: Penguin, 1991.

————. *Vita Merlini*. University of Wales Press, 1973.

Gomme, Alice. *A Dictionary of British Folk-lore*. London: Nutt, 1898.

Graves, Robert. *The Greek Myths*. London: Penguin, 1955.

————. *The White Goddess*. London: Faber and Faber, 1961.

Gregory, Lady Augusta Persse. *Visions and Beliefs in the West of Ireland*. London: Colin Smythe, 1920.

Hazlit, W. C. *Dictionary of Faiths and Folklore*. London: Reeve and Turner, 1905.

Henderson, George. *Survivals in Belief Among the Celts*. MacLehose, 1911.

Henderson, William. *Notes on the Folk-Lore of the Northern Counties of England and the Borders*. London: Folklore Society, 1879.

Hull, Eleanor. *Folklore of the British Isles*. London: Methuen, 1928.

Hutton, Ronald. *Stations of the Sun*. Oxford: Oxford University Press, 1996.

Jennings, Pete. *The Norse Tradition*. London: Headway, 1998.

Jobes, G. *The Dictionary of Mythology, Folklore and Symbols*. New York, NY: Scarecrow Press, 1961.

Keightley, Thomas. *The Fairy Mythology*. London: Whittaker, Treacher and Co., 1833.

King, John. *The Celtic Druids' Year*. London: Blandford, 1995.

Kirk, Robert. *The Secret Commonwealth of Elves, Fauns and Fairies*. 1691. Reprint, London: Folklore Society, 1976.

Knowlson, T. Sharper. *Popular Superstitions*. London: T. Weiner Laurie, Ltd., 1930.

Kondratiev, Alexei. *Celtic Rituals*. New Celtic Publishing, 1999.

Laing, L. *Celtic Britain*. London: Granada, 1981.

Larousse. *Encyclopaedia of Mythology*. London: Paul Hamlyn, 1964.

MacKenzie, Donald. *Scottish Folk-Lore and Folk Life*. London: Blackie, 1935.

Markdale, Jean. *Women of the Celts*. Vermont: Inner Traditions International, 1986.

Matthews, Caitlin. *Mabon and the Mysteries of Britain*. London: Arkana, 1987.

McGrath, Sheena. *The Sun Goddess*. London: Blandford, 1997.

McNeill, J. T., and H. M. Garner, eds. *Mediaeval Handbooks of Penance*. New York: 1938.

MS. Ashmole 1406, Bodleian Library.

Murray, Liz and Colin. *The Celtic Tree Oracle*. London: Rider, 1988.

Murray, Margaret. *The God of the Witches*. Oxford: Oxford University Press, 1970.

———. *Witch Cult in Western Europe*. Oxford: Oxford University Press, 1921

Naddair, Kaledon. *Keltic Folk and Faerie Tales*. Edinburgh: Century Paperbacks, 1987.

Nelson, Robert. *Finnish Magic*. St. Paul, MN: Llewellyn Publishing, 1999.

Nichols, Ross. *The Book of Druidry*. London: Aquarian Press, 1990.

Ó HÓgáin, Dáithí. *The Sacred Isle*. Woodbridge: Boydell Press, 1999.

O'Grady, S. H. *The Silva Gadelica*. London: William and Norgate, 1892.

Orchard, Andy. *Norse Myth and Legend*. London: Cassell, 1977.

Owen, Trevor M. *Welsh Folk Customs*. Llandysul: Gomer, 1959.

Paulson, Kathryn. *The Complete Book of Magic and Witchcraft*. New York, NY: Pentacle Press, 1970.

Peck, Arthur. *The Morris and Sword Dances of England*. London: Morris Ring, 1978.

Pennick, Nigel. *Rune Magic*. Wellingborough: Aquarian Press, 1992.

———. *Runic Astrology*. Wellingborough: Aquarian Press, 1990.

Pennick, Nigel, and Helen Field. *The God Year*. Chieveley: Capall Bann, 1998.

———. *The Goddess Year*. Chieveley: Capall Bann, 1996.

Piggot, Stuart. *The Druids*. London: Thames and Hudson, 1975.

Powell, T. G. E. *The Celts*. London: Thames and Hudson, 1983.

Rhys, A. *Arthurian Legend*. Oxford: Oxford University Press, 1891.

Ross, Anne. *Pagan Celtic Britain*. London: Routledge and Kegan Paul, 1985.

Rundle Clark, R. T. *Myth and Symbol in Ancient Egypt*. London: Thames and Hudson, 1959.

Rutherford, Ward. *The Druids*. London: Aquarian Press, 1983.

Stewart, R. J. *Celtic Gods Celtic Goddesses*. London: Blandford, 1991.

Tolkien, J.R.R. *The Lord of the Rings*. London: Allen and Unwin, 1968.

Tongue, R. L. *Somerset Folklore*. London: Folklore Society, 1965.

Watkins, Alfred. *The Old Straight Track*. London: Abacus, 1987.

Weston, J. L. *The Legend of Sir Lancelot du Lac*. London: Nutt, 1901.

Westwood, J. *Albion*. London: Granada, 1985.

Wilde, Lady. *Ancient Legends, Mystic Charms and Superstitions of Ireland*. London: Ward and Downey, 1878.

Wood-Martin, W. G. *Traces of the Elder Faiths of Ireland*. London: Longmans, 1902.

Index

☾ ORDER LLEWELLYN BOOKS TODAY!

Llewellyn publishes hundreds of books on your favorite subjects! To get these exciting books, including the ones on the following pages, check your local bookstore or order them directly from Llewellyn.

Order Online:
Visit our website at www.llewellyn.com, select your books, and order them on our secure server.

Order by Phone:
- Call toll-free within the U.S. at 1-877-NEW-WRLD (1-877-639-9753). Call toll-free within Canada at 1-866-NEW-WRLD (1-866-639-9753)
- We accept VISA, MasterCard, and American Express

Order by Mail:
Send the full price of your order (MN residents add 7% sales tax) in U.S. funds, plus postage & handling to:

Llewellyn Worldwide
P.O. Box 64383, Dept. 0-7387-0052-5
St. Paul, MN 55164-0383, U.S.A.

Postage & Handling:
Standard (U.S., Mexico, & Canada). If your order is:
Up to $25.00, add $3.50
$25.01 - $48.99, add $4.00
$49.00 and over, FREE STANDARD SHIPPING
(Continental U.S. orders ship UPS. AK, HI, PR, & P.O. Boxes ship USPS 1st class. Mex. & Can. ship PMB.)

International Orders:
Surface Mail: For orders of $20.00 or less, add $5 plus $1 per item ordered. For orders of $20.01 and over, add $6 plus $1 per item ordered.

Air Mail:
Books: Postage & Handling is equal to the total retail price of all books in the order.
Non-book items: Add $5 for each item.

Orders are processed within 2 business days. Please allow for normal shipping time.
Postage and handling rates subject to change.

LAMMAS
Celebrating the Fruits of the First Harvest

ANNA FRANKLIN AND PAUL MASON

The most obscure of the witches' festivals.

Although it has an ancient and fascinating history, Lammas (or Lughnasa) is now one of the most obscure of the eight festivals of the witches' Wheel of the Year. Celebrated in early August to mark the beginning of harvest, the name comes from the Irish Gaelic násad (games) of Lugh (a leading Celtic deity and hero).

Lammas describes the origins of the festival and compares similar festivals around the world, including Celtic, Norse, Egyptian, Russian, English, and Native American. You will find practical advice on how to celebrate the festival, themes to explore, recipes, incense, spells, traditional types of divination, and several full rituals, including a traditional witch ritual never before published.

- Discover the ancient and mysterious festival of Lammas/Lughnasa and its origins
- Explore harvest customs and witness their power today
- Learn the ancient magic practiced at Lammas
- Try out traditional recipes for food, wine, herb teas, and sweets
- Make incense to celebrate the season and invoke its powers
- Honor the gods and goddesses of Lammas

0-7387-0094-0, 284 pp., 7½ x 9⅛, illus. $17.95